HANDS ON
WEAVING

Barbara Liebler

INTERWEAVE PRESS
201 East Fourth Street
Loveland, Colorado 80537

Illustrations by Ann Sabin
Photography by Joe Coca
Cover by Signorella Graphic Arts

Contents

Introduction

I remember the first time I ever saw anybody weave. My aunt had a loom set up in the livingroom of her apartment. It was the first thing I saw when I walked into the room, and the sight was overwhelming. That big machine. All those threads. Do you really thread each one of those yarns separately? Can you really do anything on that machine without making it your life's work forever? Weaving looked fascinating to me, but so totally intimidating that I never thought about it again until about twenty years later.

What a contrast to my daughter's introduction to weaving in school! Never mind that she'd seen it all her life at home. Her kindergarten class made placemats by cutting one color of construction paper in horizontal, wavy-line strips, and another color of paper in vertical strips. They didn't make any cuts totally to the edge, so each piece of paper was held together at one edge. Then they wove the two sheets of paper together, going over one under one (a hard enough challenge for a kindergartner) to make a placemat that was then covered with clear self-adhesive plastic. Her sophisticated weaver mother thought the result was beautiful! And it was a simple, direct process with no equipment at all, using a very familiar material. To her, weaving has always been a simple and natural thing to do.

Which is the more common experience? Probably mine. Many people think weaving is a complicated activity that requires a big, expensive loom and months or possibly years of lessons. Which is the more true perception of weaving? Probably hers. Every culture in history has developed some method of weaving, and they did it with nothing but a couple of sticks and rocks and whatever plant or animal material was at hand, without even talking to each other about it until societies became more mobile. Something so universal at such an early stage of human history must be a fairly simple and natural thing in the beginning, even if more sophisticated people can make something more complex out of it.

Anyone can weave, and with any fibrous material. Just lay out some parallel fibers or sticks, and then go in the perpendicular direction across them with another fibrous material, going over-under-over-under the original parallel set. That's weaving. A bunch of reeds from the local marsh, string from your lifelong collection, hair from your girlfriend's head, wire from the hardware store, or any other fibrous material will do.

Of course weaving can get a lot more complex than that. After you've woven something with no equipment, you begin to think "If only I had a way to hold these parallel strands taut and in place, it would be so much easier to go over-under-over-under." Once you find a way to hold them taut and in place, you may think "If only I had a way of lifting every other thread so I could just slip the crosswise threads through easily instead of going over-under by hand." Or, "Pushing these crosswise threads down into place is tedious by hand—maybe I could invent a way to beat them into place automatically." Then you may think "I'd like to weave something that is bigger than this device I have for holding the threads." And so it goes, on toward complexity. Labor-saving devices are always more complex than doing it by hand—look at the modern electric dishwasher compared to the soapy water in the sink. A loom is just a labor-saving device—it is no more essential to weaving than a dishwasher is to getting the plates clean.

On the other hand, I personally am all for labor-saving devices. Thank goodness I don't have to go down to the stream to beat the family blue jeans on a rock every week. So here I am offering you a book on labor-saving devices. While it is true that you can easily weave on any piece of cardboard or any old picture frame, or almost anything else, and while it is true you can weave many beautiful things with absolutely no equipment at all, still it is also true that a little equipment goes a long way toward making the job easy and satisfying.

This book begins not at the very beginning of weaving with no equipment, but at the point of building your own simple loom inexpensively. This is not even the very rudimentary loom that only holds the threads taut—this loom does that and also makes it easy to lift every other thread so you can put the crosswise threads straight through, rather than going over and under by hand. The book then discusses another fairly simple form of ready-made loom and on to the basics of weaving on a floor or table loom. A floor loom is the big, intimidating kind of loom my aunt had. But by the end of the book, I hope you'll see that a loom like that isn't very intimidating after all.

For each of these types of looms, I'll give you a few specific projects. The projects get increasingly complex and build on each other. So please, a word to the wise on how to read this book. Please start at the beginning and read straight through to the end. The ideal would be to make each project along the way, but if you can't do that, at least please read it all and think about each process. Some things in the harness weaving chapter depend on knowledge gained in the rigid heddle chapter, and so on. We're talking about building blocks here.

After going through projects on each of these types of looms, I'll then tell you how to go on by yourself—how to plan your own project, and how to decide what kind of loom is right for you to buy if and when you decide to do that.

Step by step, we'll go through the technical details while making some neat stuff. Get your fingers ready for some hands-on learning. Weaving is fun and easy. Enjoy!

How Does Weaving Work?

Let's take a minute here to make sure we all agree on what is weaving and what is not. Weaving involves two different sets of threads, interlacing at right angles. Anything that uses only one continuous thread, like knitting or crochet, is not weaving. Anything where the elements knot around each other is not weaving. And anything that uses more than two sets of threads is not weaving—like braiding, for instance. To be weaving, it must have two sets of threads, working perpendicular to each other, and relating in some sort of over-under way.

While all those other methods of making cloth are charming and useful in their own rights, they are not under discussion here. We're talking strictly weaving.

As I said in the introduction, weaving is easy and can be done on little or no equipment. But cultures all over the globe have invented labor-saving devices to help them weave. What these labor-saving devices, or looms, always have in common is a method to keep the first set of parallel threads, called the **warp,** in order and stretched taut. That is the primary purpose of a loom.

The second most important feature of a loom, and not all looms have this feature, is the ability to lift some threads and/or lower others so that the crosswise threads, the **weft,** can go straight through instead of going over-under by hand. If you have a way to lift the first, third, fifth, seventh, etc. warp threads, then you can easily slip the crosswise weft threads across under those and over the even numbered threads. Then next you like to have a way to easily lift the even numbered warp threads so you can slip the crosswise weft thread across under those even threads and over the odd ones. This will make the over-under business fast and easy. In weaver jargon this is called **making a shed.**

Getting even more sophisticated, the common third step in loom design is to devise a way for weaving a longer piece of cloth. If you hold your warp threads straight and taut by winding them between two rows of nails on a frame, then the piece of cloth you can make is only as big as that frame. But if you devise a way to make the warp threads longer than the frame and store that extra length out of the way for later use, then you can weave something longer than the surface of the frame.

And fourth, modern commercial looms usually have a way to beat the weft threads into place quickly and easily, rather than making you push them into place with your fingernails or a comb.

Weaving—a simple over-under-over-under fabric.

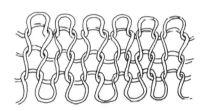

Knitting—one continuous thread looped in rows.

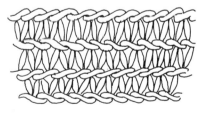

Crochet—another kind of continuous looped-thread fabric.

Those are the basic purposes of a loom, but when you go to a weaving shop and look at all the different kinds of looms, it may not seem so simple. There are several types of looms that to the inexperienced eye may look quite different. Shown here are several types: the plain frame, a simple homemade frame loom with a heddle bar, an upright Navajo style loom (which is actually a frame loom with a heddle bar), an inkle loom, a rigid heddle loom, a table loom, and a floor loom. Among these types of looms there are variations in width and style, too. And every brand is a little different.

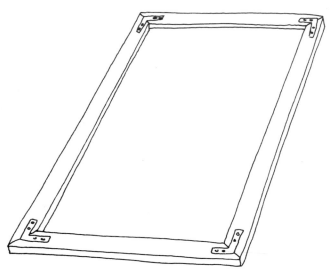

A plain frame.

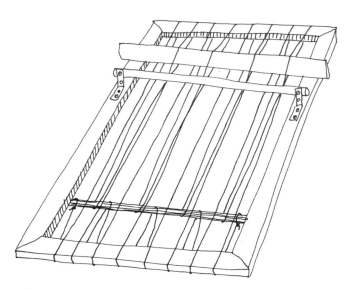

Frame loom with heddle bar.

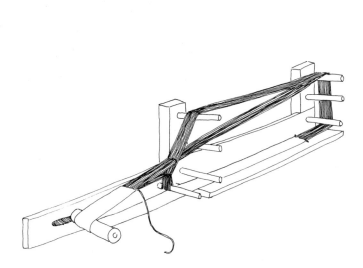

Inkle loom for weaving narrow bands.

Upright Navajo-type loom.

This may seem like a lot of different looms to learn about. But really looms are like cars—they may look a little different but actually they all work pretty much the same. They all hold the warp threads taut so that the weft threads can go over and under them to weave cloth. Except for the plain frame loom, they all have a device for lifting some threads while lowering others. Some of them have a place to store the warp yarn that is waiting to be woven, so the loom can weave a piece of cloth that is longer than the loom itself. And some of them have a way to beat the weft threads into place.

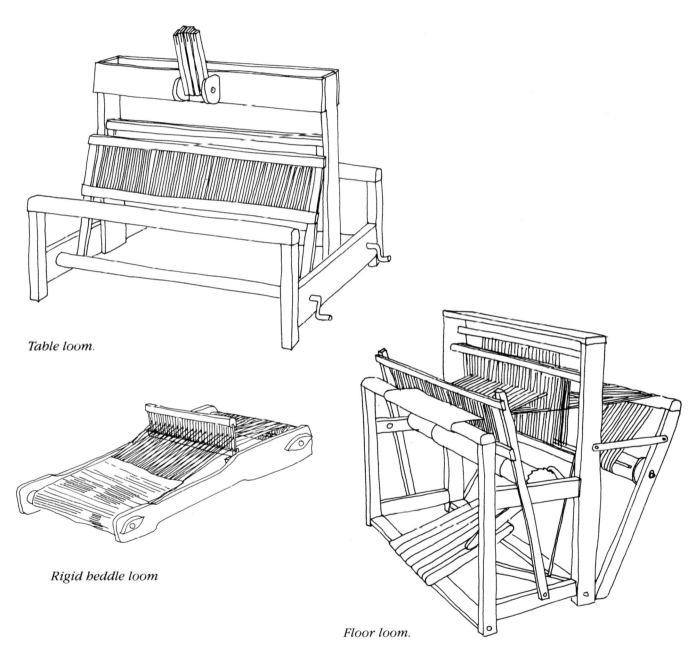

Table loom.

Rigid heddle loom

Floor loom.

How does loom weaving work? The warp actually moves from the back of the loom to the front, so let's look at the looms starting at the back. The spot where the weaver sits or stands to weave is the front of the loom.

On those looms that have a device for storing extra warp thread length, this storage takes place at the back of the loom. Usually the extra length winds around some sort of turning **beam** and can be unrolled as needed. From this warp beam at the back, the threads then go forward through some device that will lift the threads. This lifting device holds each thread individually. Different types of looms have different names for this lifting device (heddles, heddle loops, rigid heddle) but "heddle" always means the thing that actually lifts each piece of thread. In front of the heddles is where the weaving actually takes place, where the weft threads go through between the raised and the lowered warp threads. So the woven cloth builds up between the heddles and the front of the loom. If the loom has a warp beam so it can weave longer cloth, then it also needs a place to store the extra cloth that has been woven. On this type of loom, the extra length of woven cloth is stored on a rotating beam, the **cloth beam,** at the front of the loom.

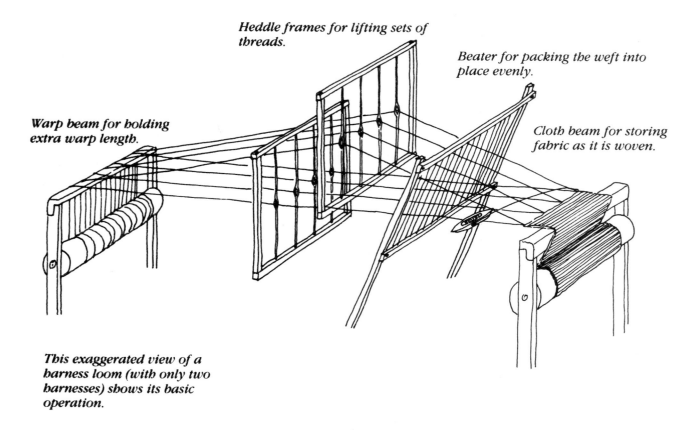

Heddle frames for lifting sets of threads.

Beater for packing the weft into place evenly.

Warp beam for holding extra warp length.

Cloth beam for storing fabric as it is woven.

This exaggerated view of a harness loom (with only two harnesses) shows its basic operation.

Those are the basics of loom operation. With those purposes in mind, you can look at any loom and see how that particular one works. Now let's get ready to actually weave our first project.

The Frame Loom

Let's start weaving with an inexpensive loom that you can make yourself, a frame loom with heddle bar. While you're at it, you can also make a stick shuttle to hold the weft yarn as you weave.

The frame loom is a simple apparatus for holding the warp ends tight. You've probably played with a simple child's "loop loom" to make hot pads, or with winding thread around a picture frame to weave. A cardboard box with the top removed and notches cut every quarter inch around the top will also make a good basic frame.

Adding a heddle bar to a frame loom makes it easier to weave faster. You don't have to go over and under each thread by hand then, as the string loops on the heddle bar will raise every other thread for you.

Building a frame loom with heddle bar

To build your loom, you'll need a few inexpensive parts. You'll need the following materials:

From an art supply store:
- canvas stretcher sides, two sides at 20" and two sides at 24"

From a hardware store/lumber yard:
- 4 flat metal corner angles, about 3" size
- 2 metal corner brackets, also 3" size
- 1 dowel, ¾" thick by the standard 36" length
- 20 wood screws about ½" long, size number 6 or 8, to attach the metal corners to the wood frame
- 2 bolts, 1" long with wing nuts, to fit holes in the corner brackets
- 3 pieces of pine lattice, 1¼" wide by 20" long each
- 2 pieces of hardwood ¼" thick, 1½" wide, and 20" or more long. 24" hardwood rulers with the metal edges removed and those edges thoroughly sanded will also work

You'll also need the following tools:
- wood drill (preferably a power hand drill or drill press)
- screwdriver
- three-corner wood file
- sandpaper
- saw
- measuring tape or rule

Start with the canvas stretcher from an art supply store. This makes a sturdy frame that is already notched to fit together firmly and easily. Twenty by 24″ should handle any of the projects shown here and still be reasonably portable.

You could also make the basic frame yourself from scrap wood instead of buying stretcher parts. If you choose to make a bigger size, use hardwood for the frame so it is strong enough to stay rigid under pressure.

Assemble the frame, either homemade or the canvas stretcher. Use the four flat metal corner angles on the underside of the frame at each corner to keep the sides rigidly perpendicular. Sixteen of the screws you bought are for this purpose.

On the top side of this frame, attach the metal corner brackets that will hold the heddle bar. This will take your last four screws. The front edge of the metal brackets should be about a third of the way down along one long side of the loom, which is 8″ down along the 24″ side if you are using canvas stretchers in the size I suggested.

Next, attach the heddle bar to this pair of brackets. Cut the dowel into two lengths, one 19½″ and the other 16½″. The 19½″ dowel will be your heddle bar. Hold it up to the top holes of the metal brackets that stick up from the frame, and mark where to drill holes so the bar can be bolted to the brackets. Drill a hole that is big enough to slip your bolts through in each end of the dowel. The heddle bar will actually be bolted onto the brackets after the warp is wound onto the loom. Test to be sure it all fits, but don't bolt the bar on yet. Now sand the whole frame and the heddle bar very well.

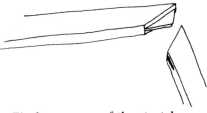

Fit the corners of the stretcher pieces together.

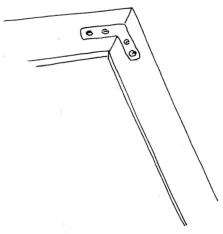

Brace each corner with a metal corner angle.

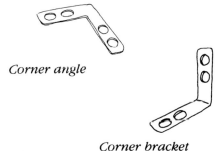

Corner angle

Corner bracket

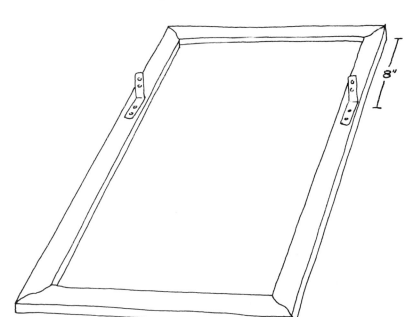

Fasten corner brackets to sides of frame. These will hold the heddle bar.

File shallow notches every ½ " across the two short sides of the loom (the 20″ sides) to keep the spacing even when you wind the warp onto the loom. These notches can begin and end 2″ in from each edge. Be sure these notches are also very smooth because the yarn must slide through them without snagging.

Now make a stick shuttle from one of the three 20″ pieces of pine lattice. Cut each end of the stick into a V-shape—that is, *remove* a V of wood so there is a notch at each end of the stick. Sand this V-shaped cut very well so it is perfectly smooth and will not snag yarn, and sand the rest of the shuttle at the same time.

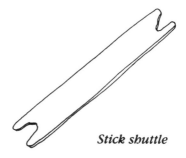

Stick shuttle

Here is your frame loom, ready to be warped.

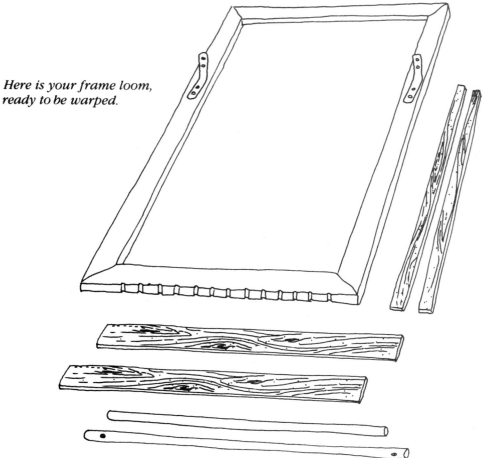

That's all for the construction phase. Those miscellaneous parts you have left are the warp end bar (the dowel), the tension sticks (two pieces of pine lattice), and the shed stick and heddle-lifting stick (the hardwood or modified ruler). Now, while you've still got your sandpaper out, sand those parts very well so they will never snag any yarn. They will be used as you warp the loom.

Starting To Weave On the Frame Loom

Now let's thread the loom and get to work on the first project. The first step is to buy yarn. How much yarn you need depends on the sett, the width of the finished product, and the length of the warp. The project instructions in this book will tell you this information, and the chapter on "Designing Your Own Project" will tell you how to figure this out on your own. But meanwhile, so it doesn't sound like Greek to you, let's go through a few definitions.

Sett is the number of warp threads per inch of width of the cloth. If your cloth will be 10″ wide and have 120 warp threads in that width, then the sett is 12 **ends per inch,** or **e.p.i.** In the project directions that follow, the sett is given.

Warp width is also given for each project. Remember that warp is the lengthwise threads, the ones that are held taut and in order by the loom. Each one of these warp threads is called an **end.** That's why sett is expressed in terms of ends per inch—it means the number of warp threads per inch of width.

And warp length is given for each project, too. This is the full length of the warp threads that you need to put on the loom for a given project.

Most weaving yarn is actually sold by the pound, not by the yard, but mail order yarn suppliers and most good weaving shops will tell you how many yards per pound there are in each type of yarn, so you can convert this yards figure to a pounds figure.

That's how to figure out how much warp yarn to buy. You'll also need to buy yarn for the weft. Weft was sometimes called **woof** in olden times. Each time the weft goes across is called a **pick** or a **shot.** How densely packed the weft is will be expressed in terms of **picks per inch** or **p.p.i.** This is the number of crosswise threads in 1″ of length of the woven cloth.

For now, you'll need just the cotton warp yarn that the first project calls for. While you're buying your yarn, also get the weft yarn: see the beginning of the next chapter for what you'll need.

Preparing the yarn

Twisted skein

Coned yarn

Spooled yarn

Yarn comes packaged up in different ways, usually cones or skeins but sometimes tubes or balls. Cones, tubes, or balls are easy to deal with. Skeins are harder. Once you develop your own sophisticated weaving studio, you'll have a **swift** and a **ball winder** to help you with this. If you don't have those things now, you'll need a willing helper to hold the skein of yarn while you wind it by hand into a ball, just like in a Norman Rockwell painting. Or, if you live in the practical modern world where spouses and friends don't do such things, you'll need the back of a chair to put the skein around while you wind it into a ball by hand.

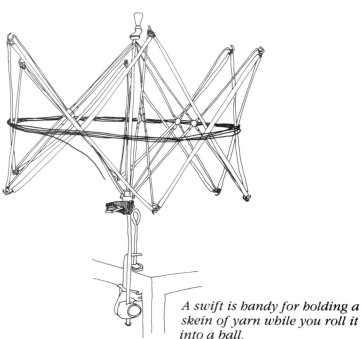

A swift is handy for holding a skein of yarn while you roll it into a ball.

A loose skein

A cone, tube, or ball of yarn will sit neatly on the floor while you pull yarn off it. If the ball or the tube won't hold still for you, try putting it in an empty peanut butter jar or coffee can. Once you have the yarn in some form that will sit neatly on the floor, it is ready to become the warp or the weft of your project.

Warping the loom

Begin by considering your project plans to see how many ends per inch you will need for this project. Remembering that the edge notches on your loom are ½ " apart, how many threads will you need to put between each notch? If you needed 10 ends per inch, you would put a thread in a notch and then four more threads before the next notch, and so on across the width you needed. The first project uses heavy cotton string for warp, and it is sett at 4 ends per inch. So there will be one warp end in each notch and one more between notches.

Also consider now how wide your project will be, and figure out how far in from the edge you need to begin in order to end up with the warp centered on the loom. Mark your beginning point on a small piece of tape on the loom. The first project will be woven 15″ wide, so mark the spot that is 7½″ to the left of the center of the lower member of the frame.

Next, there are a couple of steps to preparing the loom. Tape the 16½″ dowel, now called the **warp end bar,** to the underside of the loom about half way between the heddle bar brackets and the furthest frame member. This taping is temporary, to keep the bar from moving as you wind the warp. Then tape the two pieces of pine lattice to the back of the loom, one along each of the shorter frame members. These force the warp to be just a little bit longer, so when the weaving starts making the warp tighter, you can take them out and gain a little extra slack. These slats are called **tension sticks.**

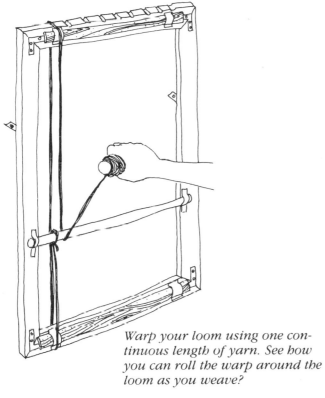

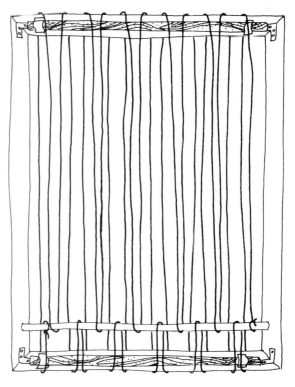

Warp your loom using one continuous length of yarn. See how you can roll the warp around the loom as you weave?

To make the warp easy to handle and to pass through small spaces, wind the warp around a stick as you would with kite string. Tie the end to the warp end bar, and begin to wind as shown in the drawing, pulling the yarn snug as you go. Remember to space the ends as you wind to get the right number of ends per inch, and to start in the place you marked with tape so your completed warp will be centered. When you've wound it all, tie the end of the yarn to the other end of the warp end bar, and cut it off the stick. Remove the tape that held the warp end bar in place. Rotate the entire warp around the loom by pushing the warp end bar down to the lower edge of the loom on the underside. This lets your weaving begin as close as possible to the beginning of the warp, so the weaving can be as long as possible. You can put a piece of masking tape across the warp threads at both ends of the loom to hold them in place until your weaving is well underway.

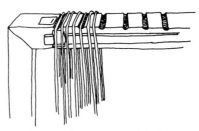

Use the notches as a guide for maintaining the correct number of warp ends per inch. This example shows 8 ends per inch.

Feel the warp to see that it is equally tight all the way across. If some spots are looser or tighter than others, pull, push, or wiggle until it all seems equally tight. Even **tension** is important in every weaving project in order to get flat cloth in the end.

The warp is now held taut at the proper spacing and even tension. This is the primary function of a loom. Now you could just put the weft in with a needle, going over and under the threads across the loom. But one advantage of a loom is that it makes a shed that separates the threads to make the interlacement faster and easier. A shed is the V-shaped space that appears when some ends are raised and some are left down. So now we'll go on to make a shed-making device.

First, let's get oriented to the new loom. What I've been calling the top side—the side that has brackets sticking up—is facing up when you weave. With the brackets as far away from you as possible, you'll have one short, notched side close to you. This short, notched side is the front of the loom. The other short, notched side is the back of the loom. The actual weaving takes place between where the brackets are and the front of the loom. It is common terminology on every loom to consider the part closest to you when you are making a shed and putting the weft through it to be the front of the loom.

The **shed stick,** one of those strips of hardwood or remodeled 24″ rulers that you made, will make the first shed. Put it across the warp between the back of the loom and the heddle bar brackets, going over even numbered threads and under odd numbered threads. In other words, go under-over-under-over across the entire width of the warp. Then, to open this shed and check that you have it right all the way across, turn the stick on edge at a right angle to the warp. After you've checked that you have no mistakes, turn it down flat again but do not remove it. This shed stick stays right there through the entire weaving process.

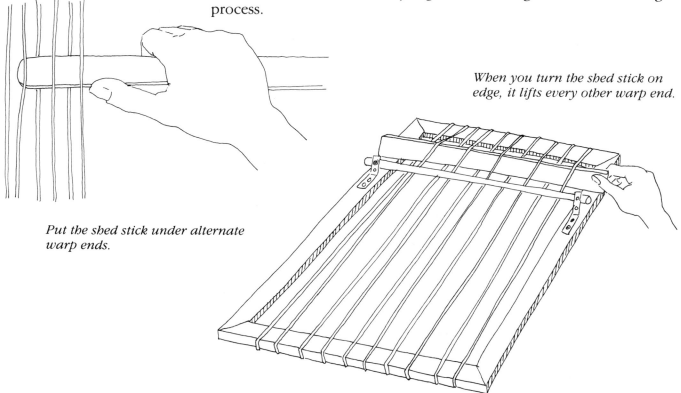

When you turn the shed stick on edge, it lifts every other warp end.

Put the shed stick under alternate warp ends.

To make the other shed, you will use the heddle bar, attaching loops of string under alternate threads in order to raise them. Cut several pieces of linen or cotton cord about 16″ long, as many as half the number of warp ends in the project. An easy way to cut many pieces all the same length is to find a book about 7½″ wide and wind around it as many times as you need pieces, and then cut the whole passle of yarn at the side of the book. These pieces of cord will be your actual heddles. Tie each cord into a loop by bringing the two ends together and tying a knot about ½″ from the ends.

You will loop these strings around the even numbered threads of the warp, those threads that go *under* the shed stick. Then the shed stick turned on edge will raise the odd ends, and the loops pulled up will raise the even ends. Starting on the right, put the first loop under the second warp end. Open the two ends of the string loop, and slip the heddle bar through these two loops. (Notice that when you lift the bar, the warp end comes up.) Work across from right to left, putting a string loop under each even numbered warp end (those that go under the shed stick) and slipping the heddle bar through the two open ends of each string loop. When all the loops are attached in this way, bolt the heddle bar to its supports.

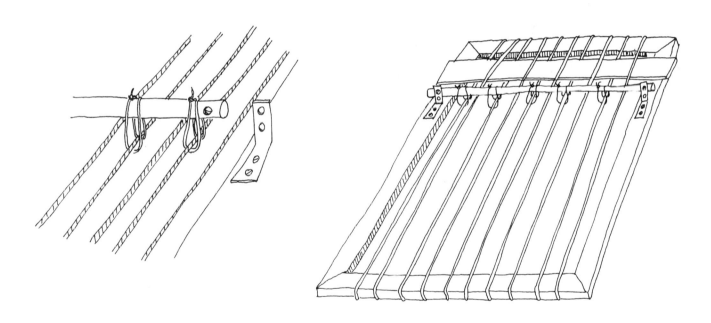

Make string loops and loop them around each warp end that the shed stick goes over. Then slide the loop ends onto the heddle bar.

Navajo weavers, who use a string heddle loom to weave their tapestries, open the shed by putting a finger under some string loops and pulling with that finger. In their weaving, the weft yarn passes under only a few warp ends at a time. But we are going to do a project where we want to put a shuttle all the way across the warp. So an easier

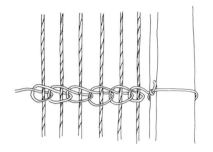

Chain a long piece of weft yarn around each warp end, as if you were crocheting. This will help keep your warp ends evenly spaced.

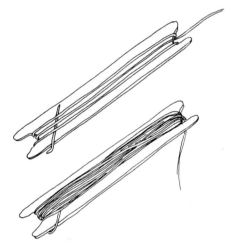

Shuttle for holding weft yarn.

way for us to open the shed, instead of one finger at a time, will be to put a stick below the heddle bar and roll it forward and up to raise all the string loops at one time. Use the loop lifting stick in this way. (That's the modified ruler or hardwood stick that is the one remaining loose part.)

One more step before you can begin to weave is to make a chain spacer. This holds the warp ends at the proper spacing and keeps them from crossing over each other, and also gives something firm to beat against when you begin weaving. Tie a doubled piece of warp or weft yarn about twice as long as the loom is wide to the right edge of your frame as close to the bottom as possible. Chain across the width of the warp as shown in the drawing, and tie the end to the frame at the left side of the loom.

Now the loom is ready to go. Look at how the loom operates while you weave a necessary first step, the **heading.** A heading is a first inch or so of weaving in scrap yarn. As you weave you'll see the warp yarns space themselves evenly and the edges pull in a very little bit. The heading gives a firm edge to beat against so the first weft shot of your finished fabric doesn't fray. The heading also gives you a chance to check and fix any threading or tension errors before you begin weaving the finished product.

So begin with a bit of scrap yarn, preferably in the same fiber as your real weaving will be. Different fibers cause different amounts of pull-in, so using the same fiber will help make the width of the heading the same as the width of the finished product. Wind it onto your stick shuttle, the piece of lath with V's cut into each end. Make your first shed by holding your stick shuttle in your right hand and using your left hand to roll the loop-lifting stick forward and up. Put the shuttle all the way across through the shed that the loops open. Now beat with a tapestry comb or a kitchen fork or your fingernails so that the weft is against the chain and forming a straight line across the loom.

Weave the next shot (with the shuttle passing left to right this time) by turning the shed stick on its edge. This will lift every other thread, the ones that the first shot went over. Put the shuttle through the shed, turn the shed stick back to its flat position, and beat the weft into place.

One purpose of the heading is to check for threading errors and even tension, so look carefully at these first two shots of weft and see if they really do maintain an over-one-under-one sequence all the way across the loom. If they don't, you will need to find the error and then correct it by re-tying the heddle loops from that point to whichever edge is closer to the error. Or maybe your error was with the shed stick, and fixing that will fix the problem. Don't bother to unweave these first two shots after you correct the error. The heading is removed at the end of the project, anyway.

When you have the order of raised and lowered threads right, weave a few more shots. Then check for even tension. See the trouble-shooting section on page 95 of this book to know how to check and how to correct any tension problems.

A Tapestry Pillow

A peaceful and rhythmic note in a harried world, this beautiful pillow will be a touch of the handmade on your livingroom sofa. Shown (on page 25) in quiet, cool colors, it could also be woven in warm or even livid colors.

WHAT YOU'LL NEED:

EQUIPMENT:
Frame loom with heddle bar warped as described in previous chapter.
One stick shuttle.
A tapestry beater or kitchen fork.
Scissors, large-eye tapestry needle.
Sewing machine (optional).

MATERIALS:
Warp: About 100 yards of heavy cotton string (about 340 yd/lb). We used Fiskgarn Mattvarp from Borgs of Lund.
Weft: Soft, thick wool yarn in pale blue, aqua and medium blue. We used Borgs' Northarsgarn (about 600 yd/lb), 1 skein each of colors 107, 100 and 74. Each skein is about 3.5 oz or 130 yd. Four-ply knitting worsted or lopi-style knitting yarn would be suitable too.
A 14"-square pillow form.
Matching thread.

PROJECT SPECIFICATIONS:
Warp: 4 ends per inch 15" wide..
Technique: clasped weft tapestry.
Finished size: 14" × 28" fabric for 14"-square pillow.

Use yarns about the sizes of these for this project.

Tapestries (fabrics with pattern shapes woven in) often use a full size line drawing of the design, called a **cartoon**, to help you keep track of the design as you weave. This drawing is pinned behind the warp, directly against the weaving, so you always know exactly where one color should join the next. To make a cartoon, use sturdy paper such as coated shelf paper, or use heavyweight Pellon® non-woven interfacing

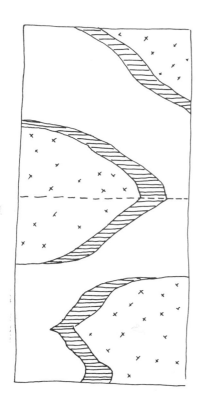

Here's a rough plan, called a cartoon, of the pillow. Use this as a guide for drawing your cartoon, or make up your own design.

from a fabric store. Pellon is very strong, and it won't tend to tear near the pin holes as paper sometimes does. Draw your design full size, to the exact size of your warp minus ¼ " on each side for pull-in. Leave a 2″ blank border at the bottom of your design as a place to pin the cartoon before you begin weaving.

You have already warped your loom at 4 ends per inch, using the cotton string called for in the materials list, and you've woven the heading. So now it is time to attach your cartoon. Place the cartoon behind the warp, with the bottom of the design even with the edge of the heading where the real weaving will begin. With several straight pins, pin through the heading and the cartoon, so that the cartoon is properly spaced right behind where you will weave.

This pillow is woven in a quick and easy variation of classic tapestry. The technique is called **clasped weft.** It involves a double strand of weft in every shot, so it produces quite a thick, substantial cloth. I've planned this project in conjunction with the next one, which is true tapestry, so that you can see the contrast between the two techniques. They use the same yarn, so you won't have a lot of odd leftovers.

To use clasped weft technique with two colors, one color must be on a shuttle and the other must be in a ball or cone that will sit neatly on the floor or table without rolling around. Wind the background color (light blue) onto the shuttle. Simply wind the yarn around from one end notch to the other until the shuttle is full.

Now take your ball of medium blue yarn and put it on the floor or on the table to the left of the loom. Pin its tail to the heading temporarily just to keep it from going where it doesn't belong. Insert the shuttle of light blue yarn through the shed from right to left, wrap it around the strand of blue yarn, and take the shuttle back to the right through the same shed.

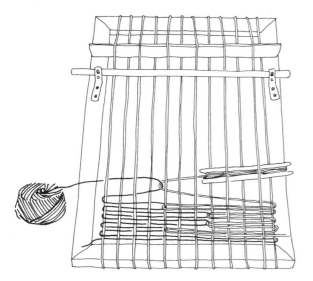

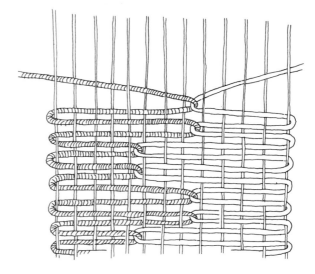

This is how the clasped weft technique lets you change color in the middle of each row.

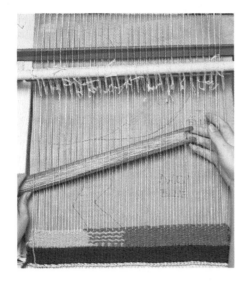

With shed stick on edge, pass the shuttle through. Loop the shuttle yarn around the darker blue yarn on the ball at your right, and pull them both back through the shed. Adjust the point at which the two wefts clasp each other to match the design on your cartoon. Beat the wefts into place.

Adjust the point where the two yarns clasp to line up with the left most line on your cartoon. Use your fork or tapestry beater to pack your wefts down snugly. Do another shot in the opposite shed, making the color join exactly above the first color join. As you beat your wefts into place, you'll see that they completely cover the warp.

Next do a pair of shots where the color join lies at the right-most line in your cartoon. Then do a pair joining at the left line of the cartoon, and so on. This alternating of where the colors join is what makes the horizontal striped areas between the solid color areas.

As you weave, you can push the cartoon up against the back of your warp to see where the lines fall, but it flops down out of your way to beat. Pin it again to the woven cloth every so often as you weave, and let it roll around the loom along with the woven cloth as you progress.

Alternating pairs of weft shots in this way as you follow the cartoon will take you half way through the front of the pillow. As your woven cloth gets too close to the heddle loops to be manageable, just rotate the entire warp around the frame to lower the top edge of the weaving.

This will give you enough room on the warp to continue weaving.

Because the weft is forcing the warp out of its straight line into slight bumps and dips as it goes over and under the weft, the warp will grow progressively tighter as you weave more cloth. When it gets uncomfortably tight, so that it is hard to open a shed, remove one of the two tension sticks that are taped to the back of the loom. This will relieve the tension so you can go on weaving.

When you get to the point where the blue area is finished and the green yarn is ready to begin, the light blue yarn on the shuttle needs to get to the other side of the warp. At that point, cut off both colors of yarn, leaving a 3″ tail hanging out each side of your cloth. These tails will be inside the seam of the finished pillow, so you can either just let them hang or work them in with a yarn needle later, following the path of the edge warp thread.

Now take the light blue shuttle to the left side of the warp and put the ball of green yarn on the right side. This puts your shuttle at the left, ready to begin the clasped weft technique from that side. Continue to weave the pillow. Notice that the cartoon includes the back of the pillow, which switches back to blue. Then the two blue sections meet at the seam, making a continuous design around the pillow.

When you have finished weaving the whole pillow, you get the joy of cutting it off the loom. This is always one of the high points of a weaver's life! Since the ends of this pillow will be turned to the inside in a seam, there are two possible ways to handle the ends. Clearly you don't want the pillow to unravel the moment you cut the warp threads. You can either machine-stitch the ends or hand knot them.

If you have a sewing machine, thread it with matching thread and have it ready before you cut the warp. Then cut warp ends in pairs, one pair about every 2″, leaving at least a 3″ tail. Tie these pairs of warp threads into knots along the edge of the fabric as anchor points to keep the fabric from immediately unraveling. Then cut across the whole warp between the end of the weaving and the heddle loops. Take the fabric immediately to the sewing machine and do two lines of a small straight stitch along the edge weft thread. Trim the extra warp ends close to the stitching.

If you do not have a sewing machine, then also cut the warp threads in pairs, but knot every pair across the entire width of the fabric at both ends. This is a permanent solution to the problem of unraveling, so do a neat and secure job.

To complete the pillow, fold it in half, right sides on the inside, and machine-stitch down one side and across the bottom where the warp ends hang out. (Enclose the header in the bottom seam so it won't show.) Turn it right side out and insert a 14″ standard pillow form. Neatly hand sew the other side closed. If you don't have a sewing machine, do all the sewing by hand. Be sure to sew a side and the warp end securely before turning it right side out to insert the pillow form.

Viola! Your first handwoven project is ready for proud display in the livingroom!

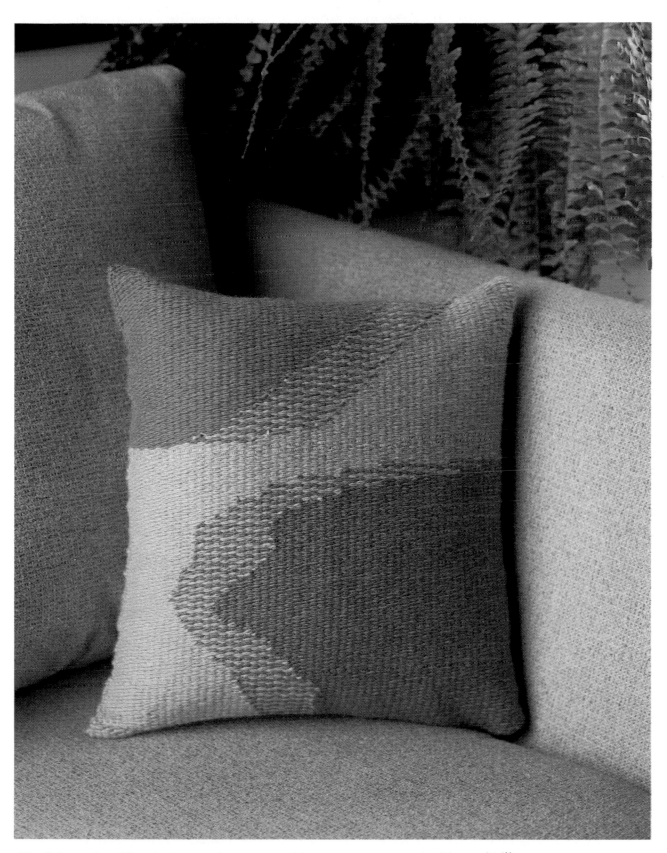

The ''clasped weft'' technique makes tapestry-like patterns easy, as in this wool pillow.

25

A Tapestry For Your Wall

Clasped weft, as we used in the pillow, is actually a quick and easy way to get the pictorial effect of traditional tapestry. But so much more is possible with true tapestry, including interesting surface textures as well as interesting flat areas. So let's go on to make a tapestry for your wall. I've planned this project to include the same three wool yarns as the pillow, with the addition of some other colors, so it could go in the same room.

WHAT YOU'LL NEED:

EQUIPMENT:
Frame loom with heddle bar.
Scissors.
Tapestry beater or kitchen fork.
A large-eyed tapestry needle.

MATERIALS:
Warp: About 100 yd of heavy cotton string (340 yd/lb).
Weft: Leftover yarns from tapestry pillow, plus one skein each of green, pink, violet and dark blue. We used Borgs Northarsgarn (about 600 yd/lb, or 130 yd per 3.5 oz skein) in colors 61, 51, 110 and 116. Other soft, heavy wools would be suitable.

PROJECT SPECIFICATIONS:
Warp: 4 ends per inch, 15″ wide.
Technique: Tapestry.
Finished Size: 14″ × 20″.

Warp your loom just like last time, using the same cotton string and again spacing your warp at 4 ends per inch. Check your threading and tension, as always, and weave a 1″ header. Copy this cartoon and pin it behind the warp.

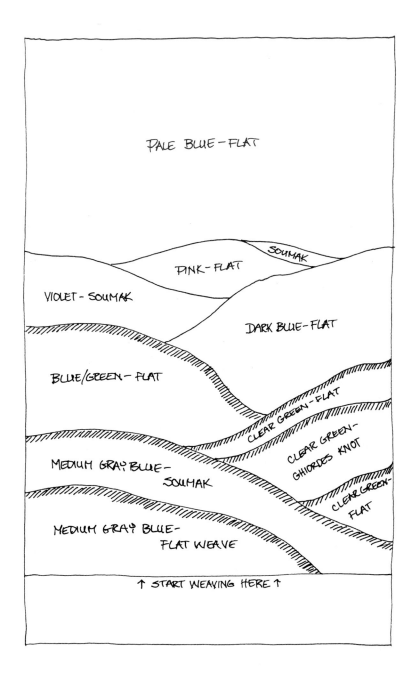

Now you are almost ready to weave, except that you need to get your weft ready. A stick shuttle is awkward in tapestry where the weft travels over only a few threads at a time; instead, use small bundles of yarn called **butterflies**. A butterfly is easily made around your fingers. Hold your left hand up, fingers outspread (assuming you are right handed—reverse if you're a lefty). Holding yarn in your right hand, start the yarn at your elbow and bring the strand up across your palm, between your thumb and first finger, and then around behind your thumb. Make a figure eight between your thumb and baby finger, going around and around until you have a moderate fist full of yarn. Clip the end with about 6″ of tail. Tie this yarn tail around the butterfly at the point where the threads cross, forming two "butterfly wings". Use two half-hitches. Half hitches are fairly easy to make with one hand, as your left hand is tied up and unable to help. After you tie the center, just slip the butterfly off your fingers and make a butterly of each of your other colors for this project. Don't make your butterflies too large, as they will be hard to put through the shed and will get tangled.

A butterfly works like a pull skein. To use a butterfly, pull on the long end that originally was hanging down to your elbow.

This tapestry uses three new techniques: interlocking tapestry joins, soumak (which is a surface interest weave that is basically flat), and ghiordes knots (which give a raised pile surface).

Look at the drawing of interlocking tapestry joins. Note that every strand of yarn is traveling in the same direction in each shed. So begin by placing each color in its own area, as defined by the cartoon, with every butterfly traveling leftt to right. Beat and change the shed. Work in the tail of each color and then take each butterfly right to left across its area. Interlock the colors as shown in the drawing.

When it is time to start a new color, note which direction the other yarns are traveling and begin the new color in the same direction. This will make it easy to make interlocking joins between all color areas.

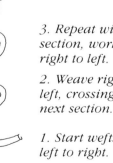

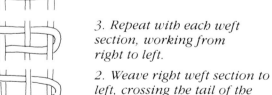

Make yarn butterflies by wrapping your weft yarn around your fingers in a figure-eight.

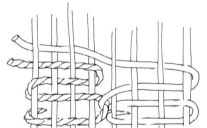

Moving a color area to the left.

Moving a color area to the right.

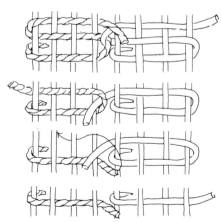

4. Do not interlock wefts when they move left to right.

3. Repeat with each weft section, working from right to left.

2. Weave right weft section to left, crossing the tail of the next section.

1. Start wefts moving from left to right.

29

Soumak is a technique for a slightly raised, somewhat different looking area. This gives surface texture and interest to the work. Note in the drawing that there are two shots of plain weave between each row of soumak. You work soumak by simply winding your butterfly around each warp end across that section, as the drawing shows. Work the soumak from your right to left shot with the shed closed, then do a straight return for your left to right shot. If you want the soumak to slant the other way, just work it on your left to right shot instead.

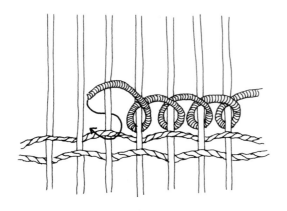

Basic soumak

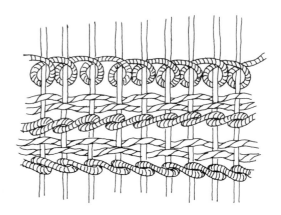

Change the direction in which you work the soumak row for a different slant.

The area that has ghiordes knots is also worked by winding the butterfly up and down around warp ends with the shed closed. Only here you must leave loops between the knots. Make these loops stick up at least an inch. When the entire knotted section is woven, plus a few flat weave shots after the knots, take your longest, sharpest scissors and trim the loops into flat cut pile. This is just like giving your son a brush cut—lay the scissors flat and cut many strands at once. It can either be trimmed flat or like sculptured pile with higher and lower sections.

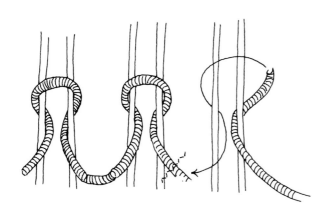

Ghiordes knots

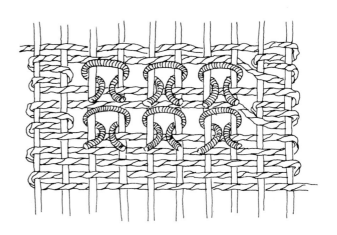

Cut the loops of ghiordes knots for a brush texture; or leave the loops intact for a different look.

Bring blue weft through the open shed (left) just to the point that the soumak area is to begin. Then make soumak wraps around each warp the rest of the way across.

When it's time to start a new color area (left), be sure to start the new weft in the same direction as the old. Ghiordes knots (right) are easy to make if you wrap the weft around a ruler or strip of cardboard to keep the loops a consistent length.

The tapestry will not have any seams to hide the ends, so you'll need to do a more presentable handworked end treatment than simply sewing with a sewing machine as you did for the pillow. The simplest technique to keep the ends from raveling is to knot the ends and work them back in. So cut the fabric off the loom with at least 4″ tails on the warp ends. Start at one edge and tie the first two warp ends into a square knot. Make it tight enough to touch the last shot of weft, but not tight enough to push that yarn out of line. Then tie ends 3 and 4 just as tight. Go on to tie each pair, being careful to preserve the straight line of the weft.

At the end where you began, you will need to unravel the header and throw it away before you tie the pairs of knots. When you have knotted across both ends, you will have a fabric that is prevented from raveling but has rather unsightly strings hanging out the ends.

Kathy Spoering weaves tiny "pocket" tapestries, only a few inches square.

Thread one end on a yarn needle and work it back in along its own path for one inch. Bring the needle out at the back of the tapestry and cut the warp thread off flush with the fabric. Put the next warp end in along its own path with a yarn needle, but make this one go about 1½". Continue to work each end back into the fabric, varying their lengths so the cloth doesn't build up extra bulk all at the same place.

An easy way to hang a tapestry while preserving its cloth-like appearance is to hang it from Velcro®. Cut the Velcro to the length of the top edge and sew one side of it to the back of the tapestry, being careful that your hand sewing thread doesn't go all the way through the tapestry so no stitches show on the front. Then staple the other half of the Velcro to your wall, and press the tapestry against it.

Other Ideas

Of course there are lots of other wonderful things to make on your frame loom, using these same techniques. The triangular shawl on page 34 simply takes a large frame, and then successive warp ends are cut and woven in as weft threads. All the other pieces shown here are possible on the frame loom you have made for yourself.

Ruth Manning's pictorial tapestries range from neighborhood scenes like this to a portrait of her kitchen shelf. Ruth uses embroidery stitches for very fine details like the water droplets and flowers.

Natural Dyes

You can weave with nature's colors—vivid golds, soft greens and tans, rich browns—by gently simmering white or natural colored wool yarn with any of a great number of different vegetable materials and a chemical mordant that helps the color "take" on the yarn. Gorel Kinersly dyed the yarns for her tapestry pillows, above, with marigolds from her garden.

The simplest procedure for dyeing yarn is the "one-pot" method. Add clean, wet wool yarn to an enamel or stainless steel pot containing dye material and plenty of water to cover. Simmer it all together for an hour or so, then remove the pot from the heat and let it cool. Rinse the yarn out well and hang it to dry in the shade.

The quantities you need for a half-pound of wool yarn are about a half-pound of dye material, and two tablespoons of alum (potassium aluminum sulfate from a pharmacy or photographic supplier), or a fourth teaspoon of potassium dichromate (available from chemical supply houses). Alum and chrome are only two of several common mordants. All are poisonous to some degree, and must be handled with care and kept away from food preparation.

Your colors will vary according to which mordants you use. Also, you can transfer your dyed yarn from the dyepot to another pot of clear water with vinegar or ammonia added; this will often change the color, making it brighter or darker. The pattern yarns in Gorel's pillows were all dyed with the same marigolds, but different mordants and additives gave her a nice range of colors to work with.

There are whole books that tell about all the different plant materials you can use for natural dyeing. A few common ones to try are yellow onion skins for rust, pecan shells for a warm tan, carrot tops for vivid clear yellow, and milkweed plants for soft golds and greens. Some dyestuffs don't require a mordant at all. Walnut hulls, sumac berries and tea leaves give good browns all by themselves. It's fun to experiment with natural dyes, and to use them in your weaving.

Charlotte Elich-McCall made a frame 6' high and 5' wide with finishing nails set ¼ " apart across the top and bottom to string her warp on. She chose a two-ply wool and a fuzzy wool-mohair blend yarn (both about 1000 yd/lb) and used them together for her warp.

For this triangular shawl, the warp *is* the weft. You just cut the first edge warp at the very top (use a push pin to keep its neighbor from falling down, too), and weave it across for your first weft shot. You can use a shed stick for one shed, and weave over-under-over-under with a big tapestry needle for the other. Beat the weft in very lightly—the fabric should look loose and open.

As you cut each warp and weave it across, you'll see the triangle shawl take shape. See how the stripes in the warp make a plaid as you weave?

Leave the loose ends hanging out, and knot them in groups of three or four for fringe. A gentle washing in warm water will fluff the fabric up. Charlotte estimates it took her about 20 hours to weave this shawl, including setting up the loom.

Opposite, from the top: Charlotte winds her warp around nails set in the top and bottom of a large frame. In the second picture, she has cut the farthest warp to the right, and is using it to weave across. She carefully beats each weft into place, not too hard. The shawl becomes triangular in shape as more wefts are cut.

The Rigid Heddle Loom

The rigid heddle loom is a little more sophisticated than the frame loom with heddle bar. It can take a long warp, whereas the frame loom could only take a warp twice as long as the frame. And it holds a nice clear shed open for you so both hands are free to handle the shuttle.

The frame of the rigid heddle loom has one important difference from the frame of the frame loom. On this loom, the front and back members of the frame are free to rotate, though they can also be held tight by a screw at the sides. Because these can rotate, you can wind a long length of warp on, so the loom can weave a long piece of cloth.

The other important difference between this and the frame loom you made is in the way the warp threads are moved to make a shed. The rigid heddle itself is a piece of wood or plastic with a series of alternating holes and slots. Each slot and each hole has a separate warp end put through it. Then when the rigid heddle is pulled up, the ends through the holes are pulled up. But the ends that are in slots will simply slide down to the bottom of the slot as the heddle is pulled up. So then we have a shed with the hole-threads up and the slot-theads down. Conversely, when we push the rigid heddle down, the hole-threads are forced down, but the slot threads simply slide up to the top of the slot. So we then have the opposite shed, with the hole threads down and the slot threads up. This gives a much smoother, cleaner shed all the way across the warp.

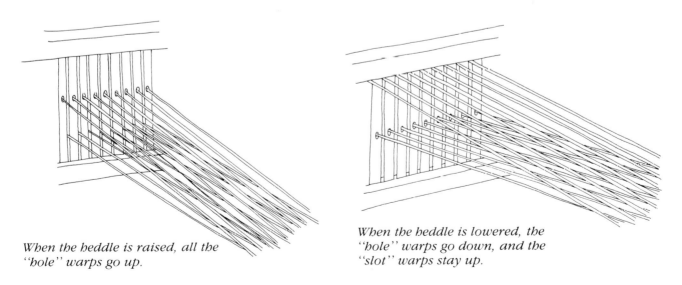

When the heddle is raised, all the "hole" warps go up.

When the heddle is lowered, the "hole" warps go down, and the "slot" warps stay up.

Rigid heddle looms come in various sizes. Choose the one that is right for the kind of things you want to weave. The largest project in this book is the evening jacket, which requires a 24″ weaving width.

Rigid heddles for the loom also come with different spacings between the holes and slots. To get a 12 e.p.i. (end per inch) fabric you will need a 12-**dent** rigid heddle—one with six slots and six holes per inch. Rigid heddles also commonly come in 10-dent or 8-dent sizes. Every project in this book for a rigid heddle loom needs a 12-dent rigid heddle. I just wanted to keep your equipment costs down at this point. If you like the rigid heddle loom, you'll want to go on to buy and use other sizes of heddles.

Let's thread the loom for our first rigid heddle project, the lacy window covering shown opposite. We'll use the lemon yellow yarn called for in the materials list on page 49.

Preparing the warp

Now let's start getting the warp ready to put onto the loom, a process called **winding the warp.** This is different from the way you put the warp on your frame loom. There you had a continuous strand of warp thread. Here each warp thread is a separate piece, called an **end.** This is necessary because you'll want to wind extra warp around the back beam so you can weave a longer piece.

To put the warp on the loom, you'll first need a certain number of threads, all the same length. Then you'll thread those ends through the heddle, tie them to the back beam, and rotate the back beam so the extra length of warp is neatly wrapped around it, ready for use when you need it. Then when the weaving builds up so close to the heddle that there's not enough room to make a shed, you'll release some of the stored warp from the back beam and wind up the woven cloth by rotating the front beam. See how this is just a sophistication of the way we rotated the warp around the frame loom?

So first of all you'll need a certain number of warp ends, whatever number is needed by the project. In the case of the window hanging, you'll need 180 ends. All these ends need to be the same length, whatever length is required by the project. The window covering directions call for a 1-yard warp length. Of course the number of ends and the warp length will vary with each project.

How do you get them to be all the same length? Not by measuring each one with a yardstick—that would take too long and leave you with such a disorganized a clump of yarn you'd never have the patience to go further. So instead you'll wind the warp on **warping pegs,** a **warping mill,** a **warping board,** or around three chairs.

Your goal is to get the right number of ends all the same measured length. So first you measure the right length on the pegs, mill, board, or chairs. From the peg where you start, or the chair back where you start, to the turn-around point at the other end, must be the right length. A

Simple finger techniques create patterns of light and shadow in this window hanging. Instructions begin on page 49.

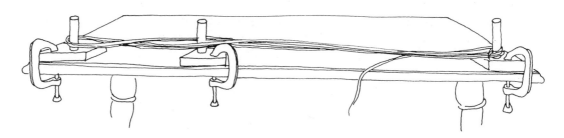

Warping pegs clamp to your table.

A warping reel makes measuring a long warp easy.

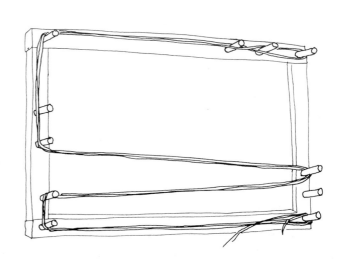

Many weavers find a warping board most practical.

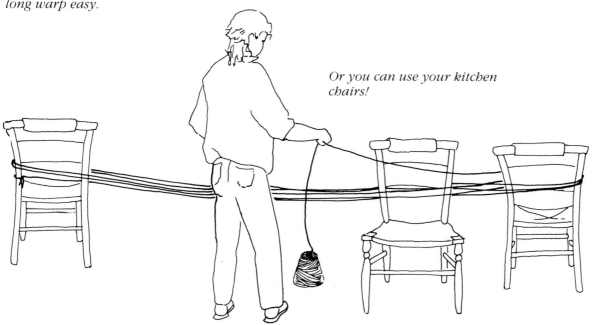

Or you can use your kitchen chairs!

few inches longer is fine if the pegs don't happen to be in exactly the right spot. Extra inches in the warp are a good insurance policy anyway, just in case you miscalculated a bit. Then from the starting peg to the ending peg, or from the starting chair to the other chair you wind the warp. When you've gone around the correct number of times, you'll have the right number of ends, all the same length. Remember that one trip to the end point is one length of warp. The trip back is a second end. You're going to cut this loop of warp at both ends.

BUT WAIT! Before you begin winding the warp, there is one more important element. Remember that you didn't just measure each strand with a yardstick partly because you'd have a big, disorganized mess to deal with? Well, if you end up with a disorganized, tangled cluster of yarn from winding this way, you won't be too much better off. Instead, you need to maintain the order in which you wound the threads so you can take them out to put on the loom again in the same order, thus avoiding tangling.

To preserve this order, you'll make a **cross** as you wind. The cross prevents each end from slipping past its neighbors, so you can tell which thread comes next as you take them out of the cluster later. The cross is basically a little figure eight that you make between two pegs of your warping device, or between two of your chairs.

First let's figure out which pegs of the board or mill to use, or how far apart to place the warping pegs or chairs. Measure a piece of scrap yarn, preferably in a different color, to the length of the warp plus 12". Tie this yarn to the upper right peg of the board or mill, or the outside edge of one chair or warping peg. Now make this yarn zigzag across the warping board, or wind around the mill, or cross the room. Where the end of the yarn is you will need a peg. See if you can move the end peg to the yarn or the yarn to the peg by rearranging things some way. With chairs or warping pegs, simply move another to the right place so the scrap yarn travels from one peg to the other, or from the outside of the back of one chair to the outside of the other chair. Now as long as you haven't wasted more than 12" of length in tying knots or whatever, this will be a pattern for winding your warp, to show where to travel with it in order to get the right length.

When you actually wind the warp, it will go from the starting point through the length of the warp, then make a cross between the two cross pegs, and then turn around the other end peg for a return trip. So let's look at the warp set up on the warping board to see which peg is which. The top right peg is the end peg. To its left, probably, will be two more pegs fairly close together. These are the cross pegs. Sets of warping pegs and some board or mills only offer two pegs at the top, so the end peg has to double as a cross peg. Working with chairs, you already have two chairs set up the correct distance apart. Now put a third chair right next to one of these so you can make a cross between these two close chairs, and then go down to the third, far chair to get the right length.

Now you can start with the lemon yellow yarn and wind the real warp. Tie your warp yarn to the beginning point, which is the peg furthest from where the cross is made. Then take the yarn along its path toward the cross pegs or chairs, following the line of your scrap yarn. When you get to the cross pegs, take the yarn over the first cross peg and under the second. (In the case of warping pegs or chairs, you'll go behind the first peg and in front of the second.) Continue to the end peg, turn around and start back. When you come to the cross pegs, once again go over (or behind) the first one you come to, then under (or in front of) the second. This makes the warp ends cross each other between the two pegs. Note that if you pull up on the first thread, it cannot pass the second because they are not parallel but rather are crossing. So they are held, at least at the point where they cross, in the order in which they were wound.

Now continue your path of yarn around the warping set-up, counting as you go. Just keep repeating going over the first cross peg you come to and then under the second, no matter which direction your hand is travelling at the time. Each full rotation, from the starting point through the cross to the end peg and back through the cross to the starting peg again, is two warp ends. When you get to 20 warp ends (10 full circuits), stop for a moment and tie a contrasting piece of string around the warp near the non-cross end. Continue, tying a **counting string** every 20 ends. If you lose count, you won't have to recount more than 20, since you just need to recount those threads not tied into a counting string. Keep winding until you have the full number of ends that you figured you needed for your warp. (In the projects that follow you don't even need to figure it out, the number is given. But if you change the plan a little, or you make up your own design, you will need to calculate the warp for yourself.)

When you have finished winding the warp, it will look pretty neat and organized. So far, so good. But what happens when you take it off the pegs? Chaos is waiting if you're not careful. So there are a couple things to do to keep it organized when you take it off the pegs. First, you need to tie the cross. This is actually just substituting threads for the pegs. Take four short pieces of contrasting string and tightly tie each of the four legs of the X that your cross forms between the two pegs. Use a bow, not a knot, but make it a firm tie so that threads don't slip out when you cut the warp at the beginning and end points. Now take some more snips of string and tie some more tight, bow-tied strings around the warp about every yard down to the end of the warp. Put the last tie about 6″ from the ending peg. These ties will keep the cluster together after you cut it.

Now you're ready for the scissors. You need to cut the warp at its beginning and ending points. The ending point is the end furthest from the cross. Cut the warp there, but do not take it off the other pegs yet.

Since we tied the warp at intervals, including 6″ in from this end, it stays together. But more organization than that would be nice, and the longer the warp the more important that organization becomes. So you can **chain** the warp to keep it organized. Begin at the end you just cut, and chain the warp. Follow the illustrations. You'll probably find this

Put ties around the cross until you're ready to actually start threading the heddle.

familiar, as most kids seem to have spent part of their childhood chaining yarn, string, or rope. The chain should be fairly loose so it is easy to unravel later. Chain up to the cross. Cut the end of the warp where it rounds the starting peg and admire your finished **warp chain**.

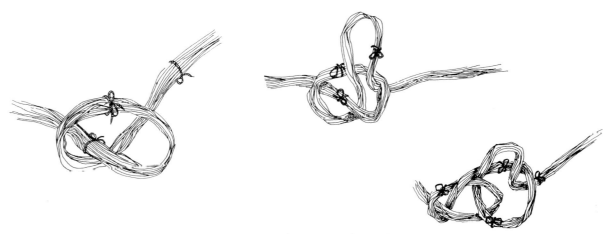

Chaining a long warp keeps it from tangling as you handle it.

Now take the warp chain to the loom and start to thread it on. This project requires 12 ends per inch, so check to be sure that your rigid heddle is a 12 **dent** heddle. Dent is French for tooth, and 12 teeth per inch to separate the ends gives you 12 ends per inch. The French are great weavers, so it's not surprising to find an occasional French word in this business.

Your rigid heddle loom will probably have some way to hold the rigid heddle upright while it is being threaded. Usually there is a slot in the frame where the bottom of the rigid heddle fits to hold it firmly upright. So find that slot and prop the rigid heddle upright. You'll be working from the front of the loom. As in the frame loom (and every other loom), the front is the place where the weaver sits to weave, which is the spot where the heddle itself is farthest away.

In order to have some firm resistance on the warp as you pull on each end to thread it, tie the warp chain to the front beam. Hold the end near the cross to the back of the loom to measure that you are leaving enough length free to thread the heddle and tie on to the back beam, then tie the main body of the chain around the front beam.

The width of the warp for this first project is 15″. How wide is your rigid heddle? How far in from one edge will you need to start in order to end up with the warp centered? Measure in that far from the right edge and put a small piece of scrap yarn through that point to mark the place.

To thread the loom, you will need a heddle hook. Some yarn supply places sell these, and most places that sell rigid heddle looms also sell them, so perhaps you already have one that came with the loom. If not, use a fine crochet hook.

Your left hand will hold the cross, not only supporting it but also preserving the order of the cross as you thread. Hold your left hand in front of you, palm up. Lay the cross end of the warp chain across your open hand and the cross itself in your palm. Then separate the short, cut parts where the ties hold them apart, and put your first finger between the two sections. One short section will then be between your first two fingers and the other short cut section of yarn will be between your first finger and thumb.

Now rotate your hand a bit so your extended fingers face toward your right hand. Open the other section of the cross that is closer to your body and leads down to the rest of the warp chain, and put your left thumb through this opening. Now your forefinger and your thumb are preserving the order of the cross, while the rest of your hand supports the warp. (This is hard to describe, but easy to do. You'll see.) You can now take off the four ties that were holding the cross.

With the heddle hook or crochet hook in your right hand, place your right hand behind the rigid heddle and put the hook through the slot or eye where you marked the beginning point. Move your left hand up close enough to the protruding hook so you can lift off the first thread from the cross and pull it through the rigid heddle. Then put your hook through the next slot or eye to the left, pick up the next end from the cross, and pull it through. Continue until all the warp is threaded. Note that the rigid heddle fills up right to left, so the ends on your left hand never have to cross over previously threaded warp, and note that you put one thread in each eye and one in each slot, threading slot, eye, slot, eye, etc.

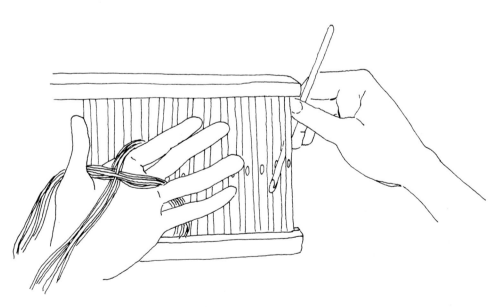

You can hold the cross on your fingers as you take each warp end off to thread it through the heddle.

Once you have threaded the rigid heddle in this way, it is time to tie the end of the warp to the **warp beam**. On most rigid heddle looms, the warp beam is the same as the back beam. The back beam on any loom is the bar that holds the warp at the proper height for weaving behind the heddles. The warp beam is always a rotating beam that stores extra warp. Are they one and the same on your rigid heddle loom?

The warp beam has some way to attach the warp, usually a row of slots to put the yarn through. Rotate the warp beam until this row of slots tilts to the back, so that yarn through the slots will not just slip off toward the front of the loom. Look at the spacing of these slots in relation to your ends per inch, and decide how many warp ends need to go in each slot. It will often be one end per slot, but don't count on it —life sometimes deals you the unexpected. Then tie two slots' worth of ends together with an overhand knot and slip the yarn into the slots so that the knot catches them there. Continue this way until all the warp ends are fastened to the warp beam.

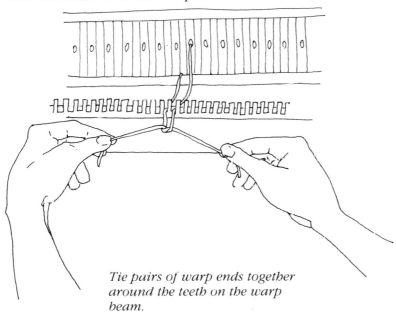

Tie pairs of warp ends together around the teeth on the warp beam.

On any loom, the warp beam is the place to wind up the extra length of warp, holding it neatly until it is time to be woven. The yarn must be wound very smoothly and neatly around the beam because even tension on all the warp ends is very important to weaving smooth cloth. So you'll have to wind the warp onto this beam carefully.

To keep all threads the same length, you need to keep each successive layer of threads separate from the previous layer. Otherwise, on the fifth rotation you may have one thread that stays on top of all five previous layers while another thread slips between to actually touch the wood of the warp beam. Then the one that slipped down would be shorter than the one that rode on top of previous layers, and this difference in length would make a loose end and a tight end as the weaving progresses. This loose end- tight end stuff makes weavers tear their hair out. It's definitely to be avoided unless you like premature balding.

To avoid that problem, simply wrap some heavy craft paper between the layers as you wind the warp around the warp beam. The paper must be stiff enough to form a smooth layer, like the stiffness of a heavy paper grocery sack. You can buy heavy craft paper at a place that sells mailing supplies, or at a paper store. Or you can cut some grocery sacks down the seam and cut off the bottom, and then iron the paper flat with a steam iron. In either case, you will need heavy paper slightly narrower than your warp beam and almost as long as your warp. It can be either in several pieces or in one long roll.

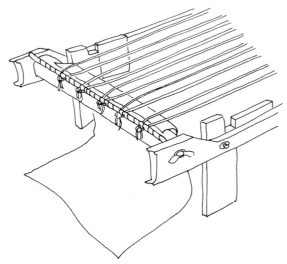

Roll stiff paper up with your warp to help keep even tension on each thread.

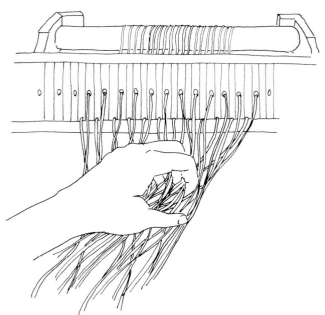

Comb the warp in front of the heddle gently with your fingers; then wind it onto the warp beam.

With the warp attached to the beam and the paper ready, you're ready to **wind on**. Winding the warp onto the warp beam is actually just an alternation of two actions, combing and cranking. First, you comb from the front of the loom. Untie your warp chain from the front beam and spread out the warp as it lies over the front beam. With your fingers, comb the warp from the rigid heddle toward yourself, pulling gently on the warp with your other hand at the same time. Comb 12″ to 18″ in front of the rigid heddle. Then lay down the warp and do not touch it while you do the other step of winding on, rotating the warp beam.

Place your heavy paper between the warp and the warp beam so that as the warp beam turns the paper will wind up along with the warp. Now loosen the screws that hold the warp beam tight, and turn the warp beam to take up the 12″ to 18″ of combed warp. Watch for tangles that will catch in the heddle and pull some warp ends tighter than the others. When the first tangle approaches the rigid heddle, stop winding and tighten down the screws again to hold the warp beam in place.

Go to the front of the loom and repeat the combing step, then back to turning the warp beam. Pull evenly on the warp as you comb, so it is snug against the warp beam as well as combed out in front. Keep feeding paper in as you wind on so that every layer is separated from all previous layers.

In this alternation process you are actually working in two ways to keep even tension on the warp. By combing, you equalize tension from one warp end to the next. By not touching the warp as you turn the warp beam, you are keeping even tension through the length of the warp. The weight of the warp is the only thing pulling as you turn, and that weight is even all the time.

Wind in this alternating way until you have only about 4″ of warp past the front of the loom. At that point you are finished winding on and are ready to **tie on in front.**

To tie on in front, start in the center of the width of warp. You're trying to accomplish two things here. You not only need to attach the warp to the loom so you can begin to weave, but you also need to make even tension across the warp.

Turn the **cloth beam**, that rotating beam at the front of the loom, so the notches are tilting slightly away from the rigid heddle. In this position, the knots will not just slip off after you tie them. Now take the center pair of warp ends, slip them through the slots they line up with, pull firmly to tighten them, and tie them in a square knot to hold them there. Next pick up the next pair of ends to the right of this pair, slip them through the appropriate slots, and tie only the first half of a square knot. Check that these ends are exactly as tight as the previously tied ends. When you believe they are equally tight, finish the square knot. Go on to tie the next pair to the left of the original pair. Keep alternating from the next pair on the right to the next pair on the left until you have worked all the way out to each edge and have the entire warp tied on, checking the tension of each knot against all previously tied knots.

Because there is slack in the warp as it rounds the warp beam, and tying these tight knots progressively pulls out some of that slack, you will find that you need to pull less and less on the warp pairs as you move from the center tie out to the edges. This is normal any time you tie on with any loom—just remember that the important thing is that the tied warp ends all feel equally tight when you pat your hand across.

Now the loom is ready to go. Look at how this loom operates while you weave the heading. Make your first shed by propping up the rigid heddle on the block that is on the inner side frame of the loom. When you prop up the rigid heddle, the ends through heddle eyes will go up, while the ends in slots stay down to form the lower half of the shed. Put a shuttle wound with scrap yarn through the shed all the way across and pull the shuttle out the other side. Now beat with the rigid heddle by moving it forward to push the weft to about an inch from the cloth beam at the front of the loom. Isn't that easier than beating into place with a fork or your fingernails? I told you looms are labor-saving devices!

Next, return the rigid heddle to the side blocks, but this time push the heddle down to hook it under the side blocks. Now the ends through eyes will be down, and the ends through slots will form the top half of the shed. Put the shuttle of scrap yarn through the shed again, starting from whichever side it now is, and beat again with the

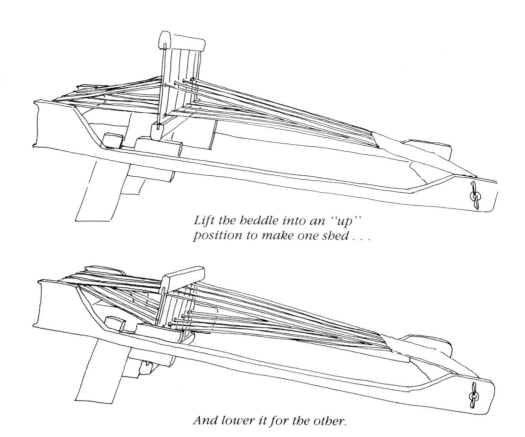

Lift the heddle into an "up" position to make one shed . . .

And lower it for the other.

rigid heddle. Continue weaving the header for about an inch, alternating the rigid heddle from the up position to the down position. Check the threading and tension, as you should at this point in any project, and correct any problems. Uneven tension can be fixed at this point by retying some warp pairs at the front of the loom. See the chapter on troubleshooting, and then fix the problem.

A Lace Hanging
For The Window

Some fabrics are most interesting for their color, some for their surface texture, some for their interesting complex structure. Let's play now with some weaves that are most interesting for the way they deal with light. This sunny window hanging can brighten up even a rainy day.

WHAT YOU'LL NEED:

EQUIPMENT:
Rigid heddle loom at least 15″ wide, warped as described in previous chapter.
12-dent rigid heddle.
1 shuttle.
Crochet hook.

MATERIALS:
Cotton or cotton-linen blend yarn that will make a balanced plain weave at 12 e.p.i. We used Cotton-lin C8/4 from School Products (1680 yd/lb, or 840 yd/8.5 oz tube), one tube each of #2 lemon yellow, #3 golden yellow, and #4 yellow orange. Cotton carpet warp would be a good substitute.

PROJECT SPECIFICATIONS:
Warp: 12 e.p.i. × 15″ wide = 180 ends, 1 yd long.
Finished Size: 14½″ × 23″.

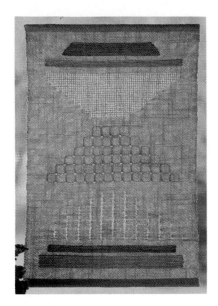

The design is limited only by your imagination in this project.

Here we are playing with different densities of fabric. The golden yellow and orange areas are more dense than the background, while the three different lace areas are less dense. And the three laces, just three of the many possible, each have a different arrangement of holes. In front of the light, these different densities are fascinating.

You already have your rigid heddle loom threaded for this project, so let's begin by making a cartoon and pinning it behind the fabric. You could also do this without a cartoon, simply counting threads to try to make the angle of the lace trapezoids match each other, but I think making those diagonal edges will be a little easier with a cartoon.

The three lace areas are made with the lemon yellow yarn as weft.

Inlay

Make a cartoon like the photo or with your own design, and pin it behind your warp. Weave plain weave background for the hem at the bottom, weaving up to the place where you want to start the inlay design. The laid-in yarn is a doubled strand of the same yarn, here starting with the golden yellow. So double the golden yellow yarn and make a butterfly of it. To weave inlay, you make a shed and put the background yarn (a single strand of lemon yellow) all the way across. Then, keeping the same shed open, put the colored yarn across only that area where you want the lay-in design to appear. Bring your butterfly up out of the shed between warps to get it out of the way. Beat and change sheds. Again, put the background yarn all the way across and then the pattern yarn only it its own area. Turn the beginning tail into this shed before you beat and change sheds. At the end of the entire inlay section, end the butterfly of pattern yarn by cutting a short tail and turning it around one thread of warp and back into the same shed as the ending pattern shot. Weave four shots of plain weave with lemon yellow, and then weave the second laid-in rectangle with a doubled strand of yellow orange. Then weave a few more shots of plain weave.

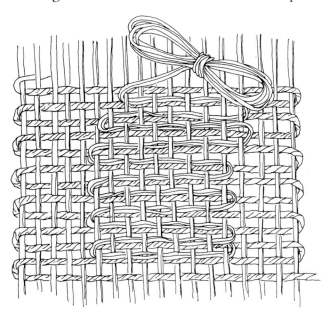

Weave the pattern yarn in the same shed as the regular weft.

50

Spanish Lace

The two-direction eyelet, also called Spanish lace, is begun by building up the border area with three shots of plain weave in the border section only. Then move the shuttle through the same three-shed sequence, weaving back and forth across the 12 threads next to one border as you build up for three shots. Beat once, not too hard, to make this section as high as your background section, then move over to weave the next 12-thread section with three shots of plain weave. Continue working sections across your pattern area, and then weave the border on the other side with three shots of plain weave. Each three-shot lace area should have ended on the same shed. Now weave three more border shots, and then work across the 12-thread sections again in the other direction. End with the three shots of weft in the border.

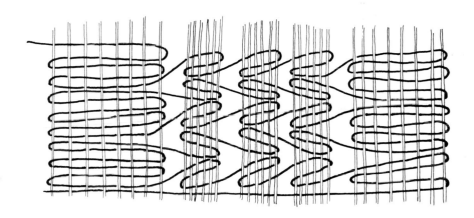

To make Spanish lace, weave back and forth across a small segment of warp, and then move on to the next segment.

Danish Medallion

The next pattern area, Danish medallion, is also worked with the lemon yellow background yarn as weft. Weave to the top of your first block of lace. Put the shuttle through the shed and bring it up between two warp ends where you want the first medallion to begin. With a crochet hook, push through the cloth between these same two warp ends but eight weft shots further down. Reach behind the woven cloth up to the point where the shuttle left the shed, and grab a loop of the weft yarn as it comes off the shuttle. Pull this loop below the woven cloth and up through the fabric at the point where the crochet hook entered the cloth. Pull up a big loop and pass the shuttle through this loop. Then pull on the thread where it leaves the shuttle until this loop pulls together the cluster of eight weft shots and an eyelet is formed. Then pass the shuttle again through the same shed past ten or so warp ends and up out of the shed. Again pull up a loop in the same way.

Repeat this across the pattern area. For the next row of medallions, weave eight shots of plain weave and begin the sequence again, starting the medallions one block farther in. After weaving all your rows of medallions, weave a few shots of plain weave.

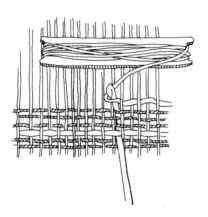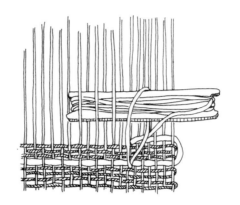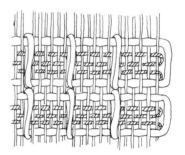

Danish medallion

Leno

One-over-one eyelet is also know as leno weave. It is most easily worked with a pick-up stick. Your shed stick from the frame loom will make a good pick-up stick. Build up the border area two weft shots high. Open a shed and put the stick through from the left, over to where the pattern area is to begin. With your right hand, twist the next two warp ends and push the stick through this twist to hold it. Then twist the next two warp ends and push the stick through. Do this across the pattern area, then push the stick the rest of the way through the open shed in the background area. Turn the stick on edge to make a shed and put the shuttle through just in front of the stick. Remove the stick and beat. Guild up the border on that side two shots high. Now make the opposite shed with the rigid heddle and put a shot across. Repeat the pattern technique with the stick for the next shot, building up the border area with two shots of plain weave for each shot of leno in the design area.

To weave leno, twist pairs of warps around a shed stick. Then turn the stick on edge and put the weft through the shed it makes.

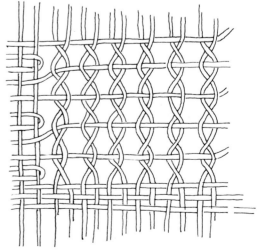

52

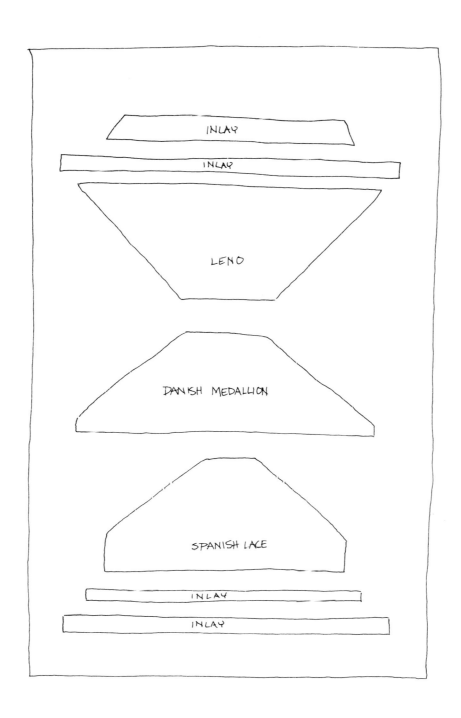

A rough sketch like this, made to size and pinned behind your warp, serves as a guide to placing pattern areas.

Follow your cartoon to make the remaining inlay areas. Weave enough plain weave at the top to allow for a hem. Machine stitch the ends when you cut it off the loom, to prevent unraveling.

Hand wash the finished fabric as you would a fine sweater, drying it flat and ironing it when it is nearly dry. Washing is an important finishing step for most fabrics except tapestry. It lets the threads in both warp and weft relax and settle in in relationship to each other, and it **fulls** the yarns. That is, it lets them fluff up to their true size and shape.

To finish your window hanging, you'll need two thin metal rods from a hardware store and some heavy-weight nylon fishing line. Buy the clear, nonreflective type of fishing line. Roll the end of the fabric around the metal bar that has been cut to the right length. Hand-hem the fabric around the bar, stitching the ends closed as well so the bar doesn't work its way out. Thread some fishing line onto a large-eyed needle, and put it through the fabric to knot around the top bar 1″ in from one end. Measure how long you need the hanging string to be, and then knot it around the bar at the other end.

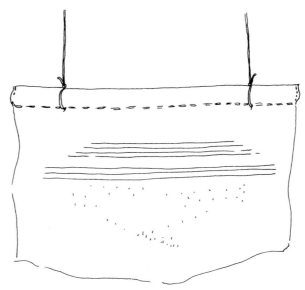

Hang it in a sunny window and enjoy!

Upholstery Fabric

Color and surface interest are the outstanding design features of the upholstery fabric on page 57. Though we are still working with basic plain weave, where each thread in either direction goes over-one, under-one, here we see that varying the yarns in the warp and the weft will give an interesting surface.

The design here is purely a result of the order of yarns in the warp and the weft. This is the first project where we have used more than one type of yarn in the warp. Rather than describing verbally how to do this, the standard way to indicate a threading is with a **draft**. A draft is a symbolic representation of warp and weft threads. It is drawn on graph paper. There are several variations in the way people write drafts, so drafts in different weaving books may look a bit different. But the basic method is the same.

There is a horizontal bar to the draft, and each square on this bar is a heddle. For the rigid heddle loom, that means that each square of the graph is either an eye or a slot. The rows of graph paper in this horizontal bar are groups of threads that work together. So on a rigid heddle loom, the top row may be the slots and the bottom row the eyes, or vice versa. On a harness loom, which we will get to later in the book, there are four rows of squares for the threading if we are using a four harness loom, because there are four groups of warp ends that work together. A rigid heddle has only two groups—the eyes group and the slots group. (They probably have those same two groups in Las Vegas.) On the draft given here, the upper row is the slots and the lower row is the eyes.

A draft also has a vertical column. This part tells you what to do with the weft. Note that this draft indicates two different sheds by having two different columns. At the corner where the horizontal and vertical parts meet, the draft tells how the manipulation of the heddles goes with the weft. An X in this corner area means that this group of threads is raised. For a rigid heddle loom, the only two possibilities are to raise the eye threads or to raise the slot threads. So there are only two possible Xs in the corner, and there are only two columns below those Xs.

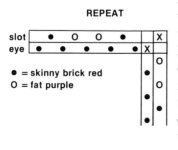

Looking at the draft for this particular fabric, we see that we are using two different yarns in the warp. These are indicated by a small dot and a larger circle simply because one yarn is very fine and one yarn is fat; any other symbols would also do. So we need to thread three skinny ends, going eye-slot-eye, then a fat end in the slot, a skinny in the eye, and a fat in the slot. Then we repeat this pattern across. So let's go ahead and do this, and come back to the weft part of the draft when we're ready to weave.

WHAT YOU'LL NEED:

EQUIPMENT:
Rigid heddle loom as wide as your fabric needs to be (ours is 20″).
12-dent rigid heddle.
2 boat shuttles and a bobbin winder, or 2 stick shuttles.

MATERIALS:
Fine wool yarn about 2000 yd/lb. We used Harrisville Designs singles (440 yd/3.5 oz skein), 3 skeins of brick #108. Heavier wool yarn, about 500 yd/lb. We used Harrisville Designer Yarn (250 yd/8 oz cone), one cone of blue-violet #128.

PROJECT SPECIFICATIONS:
Warp: 12 e.p.i. × 20″ wide = 240 ends, 2 yd long.
Technique: Surface-interest plain weave.
Finished Size: 18″ × 44″ with a 6″ sample.

First, wind two separate warps, one of skinny brick red yarn and one of fat purple yarn. There are 240 ends in the entire project, and we can see by the draft that 2/6 of them will be fat purple and 4/6 of them will be skinny brick red. So that makes a total of 80 ends of fat purple and 160 ends of skinny brick red. They each need to be 2 yards long. So wind two separate warps of these two yarns.

When you are threading two or more different yarns on a loom, you will thread one whole warp chain leaving empty spaces for the other yarn(s). It is much easier to count filled spaces than empty spaces, so always thread the yarn with the most ends first. In this case that would be the skinny brick red yarn. Thread the loom, leaving an empty slot each time there should be a fat purple. Then go back and fill these

This fabric looks complicated, but it's a simple plain weave with alternating fat and thin threads in both warp and weft.

The table runner above has heavy jute threads at intervals in the warp and weft, with leno twists between them, The runner at left is plain weave with gaps left in both the warp and weft for an open, lacy look.

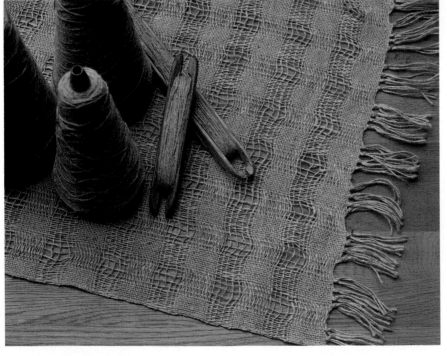

slots with the fat purple warp. This particular fabric depends greatly on having all the fat purple yarns in slots only, never in eyes, so be careful about that.

Wind on with paper between the layers as you learned in the last chapter, tie on in front and weave a heading while you check the threading and tension.

So far we've used butterflies or a stick shuttle, but in a fabric where the shuttle travels across the whole warp, and especially when there is more than one weft yarn, it is easier to use boat shuttles. These are another labor-saving device. You can buy them from a weaving dealer, either locally or by mail order. You'll need to buy some bobbins and a bobbin winder too if you buy boat shuttles. Use the bobbin winder to wind the bobbins as the drawings here show, so that you have one bobbin of skinny brick red yarn and one bobbin of fat purple yarn. Of course stick shuttles would also do the job—boat shuttles are just easier and more satisfying to use.

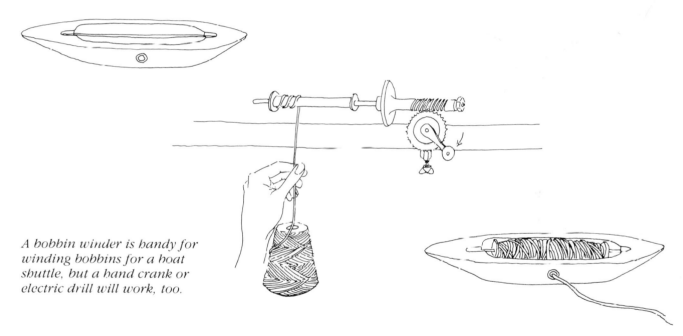

A bobbin winder is handy for winding bobbins for a boat shuttle, but a hand crank or electric drill will work, too.

Now you're ready to start weaving, so let's look at that draft again. The vertical column indicates what to do with the weft. This is really easy to remember if you think of the draft as a map of your loom. The heddles are in a horizontal line in front of you as you sit at the front of the loom. So it makes sense that the horizontal line represents the heddles, and each vertical column of two squares in that horizontal bar represents one warp end. Any one warp end can go through either a slot or an eye but not both, so there is never a mark straight above or below another mark. The cloth builds up vertically from close to further away, so it makes sense that the vertical column of the draft represents how you build up the cloth with the weft. The horizontal rows of two squares within this vertical column each represent one weft shot. A weft shot can be in one shed or the other but never both at once, so there is never a mark straight beside another mark.

Read the treadling draft from bottom to top, just as your fabric builds up from bottom to top, So the first thread in this draft is a skinny brick. The top of that column indicates that the eyes are raised for this shot. The next shot, reading up from the bottom, is a skinny brick with the slots up. Note that the yarn order in the weft is the same as in the warp. That's all you need to know to weave the whole cloth.

When you've finished weaving enough fabric to cover your chair seat, take a couple of inches to weave yourself a sample of a coordinating fabric. For this fabric, use only the skinny brick yarn for the weft. You'll see another fabric with a vertical rib. This would coordinate very well with the fabric you just wove. Do you have another chair to cover?

Finish the ends with a tight, straight machine stitch since they will not show. The fabric should then be machine-washed with Woolite for three minutes in cool water to full the fabric, dried flat and pressed with a damp towel over it. Cover your chair with the finished fabric.

An Elegant Evening Jacket

Did you think you couldn't weave clothing if you didn't have a 45″ wide loom? Many people think that, simply because commercial fabric is almost always that wide and commercial clothing pattern layouts are designed for that width.

When I was first learning to weave and working on borrowed or rented looms, I had a 20″ wide loom and a burning desire to make clothing. I had done some professional tailoring, back in the days of my youth when my patience was high and my time was free. So I was especially used to thinking of clothing fabrics as being 45″ wide. But when I measured every commercial pattern I had and found the widest piece to be only 17″ wide, I decided to throw that notion out the window.

I now know that garments of all kinds can almost always be made of pieces from the narrowest loom. Where there's a will there's a way, and some of the most innovative designs I've seen have come from the necessity of using a small loom to make a big project.

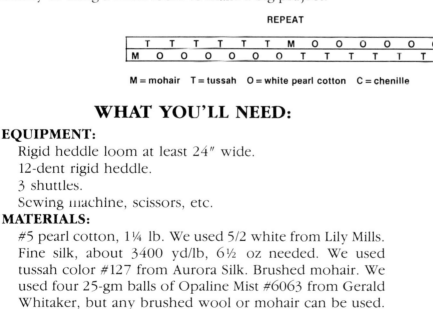

REPEAT

T	T	T	T	T	M	O	O	O	O	O	X
M	O	O	O	O	O	T	T	T	T	T	X

M = mohair   T = tussah   O = white pearl cotton   C = chenille

Right column (top to bottom): X, T, C, T, C, T, C, T, C, T, C, T, C, M, T, C, T, C, T, C, T, C, M

WHAT YOU'LL NEED:

EQUIPMENT:
Rigid heddle loom at least 24″ wide.
12-dent rigid heddle.
3 shuttles.
Sewing machine, scissors, etc.

MATERIALS:
#5 pearl cotton, 1¼ lb. We used 5/2 white from Lily Mills. Fine silk, about 3400 yd/lb, 6½ oz needed. We used tussah color #127 from Aurora Silk. Brushed mohair. We used four 25-gm balls of Opaline Mist #6063 from Gerald Whitaker, but any brushed wool or mohair can be used. Heavy cotton chenille, about 900 yd/lb, 1 lb. We used "Baby Bear" from Henry's Attic.

PROJECT SPECIFICATIONS:
Warp: 12 e.p.i. × 24″ wide = 288 ends, 3¾ yd long.
Technique: Log cabin weave.

This beautiful evening jacket by Betty Davenport uses color order in both the warp and weft to create the surface design. This type of fabric design is called log cabin, and it is one of many pattern effects that can be made by special arrangement of color in the warp and weft.

It uses Simplicity Pattern #7695, but other similar styles could be used. Do any adjustments to the pattern and lay it out to be sure of the size of fabric you will need. The size of finished fabric used for this jacket was 21″ × 3 yd 6″. There was 7% shrinkage in the warp direction after weaving and washing.

Modify the pattern pieces to make room for the crochet edging by cutting 1″ inside the sewing line around the neck, front, and bottom edges and around the bottom of the sleeves. Modify facings in the same way. Cut iron-on interfacing to the shape of the neck and front facings.

Log cabin makes its pattern of vertical and horizontal blocks of stripes through clustering the colors in the warp. Note that in the draft, one block has the brown flecked yarn only in the slots. In the next block, the brown flecked yarns are only in the eyes. Because the colors operate together in groups, they make stripes.

Thread a 3¾ yd warp onto your loom as the draft shows, and weave the whole length of the warp according to the draft for the weft order.

To finish the fabric, machine stitch the ends and hand wash it. Dry flat, stretching occasionally. When nearly dry, lay it on a terry towel with a damp press cloth on the back and barely touch the iron to the press cloth. Remove the press cloth and lightly fluff up the chenille with the flat of your hand.

Sewing with handwoven fabric is a bit different from sewing on commercial fabric because handwoven fabrics often fray more easily. There are a couple of different ways to deal with this problem. One way is to lay out the pattern pieces and draw around them with a washable marker without cutting. Then machine stitch inside the cutting line before actually cutting out the piece. This keeps the edges from fraying or stretching as you sew, as they would if you cut first and stitched the edges later. The other possibility is to cut out the pieces and, before you move them at all, treat all edges with Fray Check®, a fabric glue that comes in a squeeze bottle.

Cover all interior seams with seam binding in a matching or complimentary color. Iron on the fusible interfacing to the facings and finish the inside edges of the facings with seam binding. Stitch the facings to the jacket, wrong sides together, close to the edge. Cover this machine stitching with the first row of crochet. Use the chenille yarn to do the crocheted edge, starting at the lower side seam with a row all the way around of single crochet. Work three more rows in half double crochet, increasing three to six stitches at corners and one stitch at the center front curve. Decrease one stitch at each side of the inside neck curve. Finish the ends of the sleeves with the same crocheted edging.

That's all there is to it!

This is a plain weave fabric, too! The pattern effect comes from alternating different colors and weights of yarn in both warp and weft.

One long, narrow rectangle, cut into four sections and seamed together, shapes this simple top.

Clothing Without a Pattern

For people like me who came to weaving after life as a seamstress and tailor, the concept of clothing from a few rectangles is amazing. But the history of clothing throughout the world shows this to be a much more basic and much older idea than our modern system of many pattern pieces with complex shapes. In fact, it is interesting to note that you can tell whether a culture has been a weaving culture or a fur culture by the shape of their traditional garments. If the garments had curved lines, like the 18th century Manchu dynasty coat sketched here, then it was a fur culture. The pieces of this garment are the shapes that fit efficiently on a pelt, but would waste an awful lot of fabric if placed on a rectangle of cloth.

Where the traditional garments are composed of rectangles, perhaps with a few triangles for fit, we know the culture was a weaving culture. This 18th century Spanish man's shirt hardly wastes an inch of fabric, even though it is a fairly complex design. Rectangles are the most efficient shape for using handwoven fabrics, while they are extremely inefficient for cutting fur pelts.

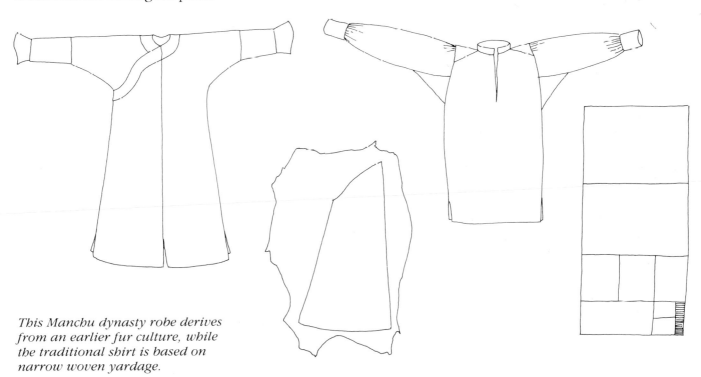

This Manchu dynasty robe derives from an earlier fur culture, while the traditional shirt is based on narrow woven yardage.

Modern commercial patterns are inefficient in their use of fabrics. Quite a bit of cloth is scrap, whereas traditional garments of woven cloth were designed to use every square inch of fabric. This shows that we have cheap cloth, machine made in vast quantities rather than laboriously hand made. We can afford the luxury of being wasteful!

Here is a striking garment that takes only 135″ of 9½″ wide fabric. It is made completely of rectangles, so not a single square inch of your precious handwoven fabric is wasted, except for the neck hole.

WHAT YOU'LL NEED:

EQUIPMENT:
Rigid heddle loom at least 12″ wide.
12-dent rigid heddle.
1 shuttle.
Large-eyed embroidery needle.
Sewing machine, scissors, thread.

MATERIALS:
This top uses a combination of weights, textures and colors of yarn in the warp. We used the following Crystal Palace yarns in the warp: 190 yd of Belle Ecosse (mercerized cotton cord, 860 yd/lb) in purple; a pound of Luxor (mercerized cotton, 1000 yd/lb) in natural; 300 yd of Chenille Coton (cotton-rayon blend, 1100 yd/lb) in magenta; and 200 yd of Country Ribbon (cotton, 800 yd/lb) in gray. Our weft is fine 30/2 cotton from Borgs of Lund, 3300 yd/lb, in natural.

PROJECT SPECIFICATIONS:
Warp: 12 e.p.i. × 12″ wide = 144 ends, 5 yd long.
Technique: Warp-predominant plain weave.
Finished Fabric Size: 9½″ × 3¾ yd.

This will be the first fabric we've made in warp predominant fabric, so let me tell you a bit about the balance of the fabric.

The first two projects we did, the pillow and the tapestry, were **weft faced** fabrics. This means the woven fabric showed weft only; the string we used as warp didn't show at all in the finished fabric.

The three projects we've done so far on the rigid heddle loom have been **balanced** weave, where the warp and the weft show equally. Most commercial fabrics are balanced weaves—look at any shirt in your closet as an example.

We have not done a weft predominant fabric, but you can imagine a fabric between balanced and completely weft faced, in which the weft predominates on the surface but there is a bit of warp showing.

Warp predominant fabric, then, must be fabric in which the predominant look is the warp (even though the weft shows a bit), and warp faced fabric has only warp showing on the surface. So we have a continuum here: weft faced, weft predominant, balanced, warp predominant, and warp faced. Any fabric falls somewhere in this continuum.

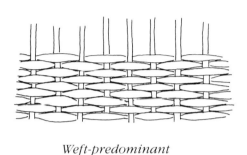

Weft-predominant

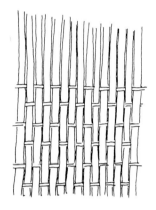

Balanced plain weave

Warp-predominant

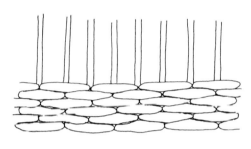

Weft-faced

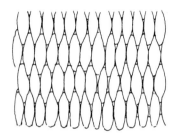

Warp-faced

Any weave structure can be any of these degrees of balance. So far the only weave structure we have dealt with has been plain weave, where every thread goes over-one-under-one at all times, but we have seen it in both weft faced and balanced ways. This striped top is also in plain weave, but it will be our first experience with warp predominant fabric. It is a good example of why one might choose to make a fabric warp predominant.

Notice that this fabric has a lengthwise stripe. That is a stripe in the warp direction, so you could guess that it is made by putting different colored yarns in the warp. Good guess. But then if we weave that pretty striped warp so that the weft is dominant, or even so the weave is balanced, the stripes will get partially obliterated. So instead we accent the stripe by downplaying the weft. In this case we'll accomplish the warp predominance by using a skinny white weft that holds the cloth together without covering the warp stripes any more than necessary.

Warp faced fabrics, because the threads must be packed so tightly, tend to be too stiff to make good clothing. The pillow and the tapestry were tightly packed in the weft, and remember what a firm fabric they made? So warp predominant fabric is a compromise between our wish to have the stripes show and our wish to have fabric that drapes enough for clothing.

Thread your rigid heddle loom at 12 e.p.i. with the color order given in the draft. Remember that it is easier to thread your predominant color first and then fill in the empty spaces with the other color. Weave the whole warp with the thin white yarn, taking care to beat lightly.

Machine sew the ends of the finished fabric and wash it by hand in warm water. Dry flat, and press when nearly dry. Your finished fabric will be about 9½″ wide.

Mark and sew the ends before cutting the fabric into four lengths: two pieces at 38″, one piece at 38½″, and one piece at 20½″. Place the two 38″ pieces edge to edge with the color areas to the center and sew a seam. This is the top front and back and the sleeves. Mark the neckhole and sew around it before cutting. The hole is 6″ wide, extending 1″ back from the seam and 4″ to the front from the seam. Try it over your head to be sure it fits, then finish with a buttonhole stitch using the thick white yarn to cover the machine stitching.

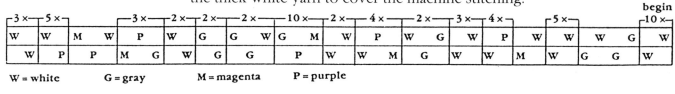

⌐3×¬	⌐5×¬			⌐3×¬	⌐2×¬	⌐2×¬	⌐2×¬	⌐10×¬	⌐2×¬	⌐4×¬	⌐2×¬	⌐3×¬	⌐4×¬		⌐5×¬			begin ⌐10×¬
W	W	M	W	P	W	G	G	W	G	M	W	P	W	G	W	P	W	W	W	G	W
	W	P	P	M	G	W	G	G	P	W	W	M	G	W	W	M	W	G	G	W

W = white G = gray M = magenta P = purple

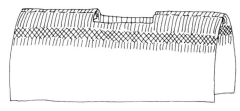

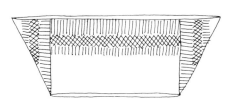

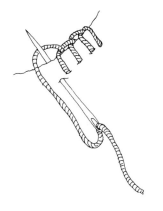

*Fold and stitch your strips like this
for a comfortable, easy top.*

Place the end of the 20½″ piece against the side of the 38½″ piece as shown in the drawing and sew a seam. Turn the other end of the long piece around the back to meet the end of the short piece as the drawing shows, and sew a seam there. This is the bodice. Attach it to the neck and sleeve piece with two long horizontal seams, front and back. Finish the sleeve ends with a buttonhole stitch like the neck edge and wear it with pride.

The Four Harness Loom

The rigid heddle loom made a few things easier than the frame loom, didn't it? You could make a shed more easily and you could weave longer cloth. It was easier to beat, too.

The biggest difference between a frame loom and a rigid heddle loom is in making those physical operations easier. The main advantage of a harness loom over a rigid heddle loom is in the complexity of fabric structures that can be easily made. With a rigid heddle loom, you can only go over-one-under-one. You can only make plain weave. (Actually there are techniques for doing more complex things by using more than one rigid heddle or by using a pick up stick, but they are beyond the scope of this book.)

A rigid heddle loom has only two groups of threads, those in the slots and those in the eyes. A harness loom has as many groups of threads as it has harnesses. Every heddle is controlled by one of the harnesses, making the heddles work together in groups. On a 4-harness loom, there are four different groups of threads that can be operated in any order. On an 8-harness loom there are eight groups, and a 20-harness loom has 20 groups. These groups of threads are usually operated in combinations. For example, on a 4-harness loom one of the simplest orders of operation is to raise harnesses 1 and 2 for the first shed, then 2 and 3 together for the second shed, then 3 and 4, then 4 and 1. So it is not only the greater number of groups of warp ends, but also the number of possible combinations, that make so many complex patterns possible.

How does the loom know which ends to raise to make the pattern you want for your cloth? Good question. It knows because you have threaded the heddles in a pattern of your choice. Each warp end goes through only one heddle on the particular harness called for in your threading draft. Then as you put in the weft, you open the shed with the combination of harnesses called for in your draft.

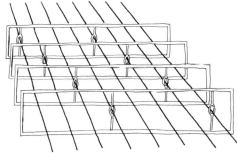

Each warp thread goes through one heddle. The order in which you choose harnesses for each successive thread determines your woven pattern.

The harnesses are connected to **treadles** at your feet on a floor loom or **levers** on your table loom. You connect whichever harnesses you want to treadle 1, another set of harnesses to treadle 2, etc. as called for in the corner of your draft. Then you step on the right treadle or move the right lever to raise harnesses 1 and 3. For the next shot you raise harnesses 2 and 4 by using the appropriate treadle or lever. Or you could raise harnesses 1 and 2 for the first weft thread and then 3 and 4 for the next weft thread, creating a different pattern in your cloth.

So here again the individual looms differ, but the principle is the same. The threading pattern, the tie up, and the order of lifts in the treadling let you make different patterns in the cloth.

Before we get into looking at how these more complex patterns are achieved, lets take a brief walk-through of the physical differences between this loom and the ones you are already familiar with.

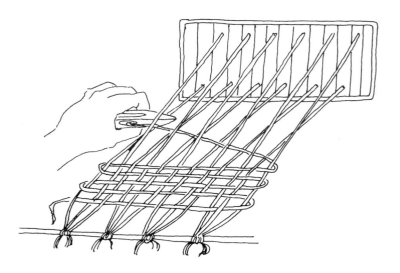

Raising different harnesses or combinations of harnesses creates different sheds.

Starting at the back (since that's where the cloth actually starts), we see that a floor or table loom has a warp beam that is separate from the back beam. The purpose of the warp beam is to hold the extra length of warp in a tight, neat way. The warp beam has a brake on it to hold it tight, and some way to release that brake when you want to wind forward. On a floor loom, there is usually a brake release pedal that reaches to the front of the loom so you can operate it without leaving your seat.

Above the warp beam there is a stationary back beam. Its purpose is to hold the warp at the proper height for the harnesses to operate well.

In front of the back beam are the harnesses. This is a 4-harness loom, so you see four frames (harnesses) that can slide up and down. Attached to these harnesses are the heddles that will actually hold each warp end. Each warp end is through a heddle on only one harness. The harnesses are lifted, alone or in combination, to make the shed.

This lifting is accomplished by operating the treadles that are below the harnesses. Different treadles are tied to different harnesses. On a table loom, the harnesses are attached to levers that are hand operated rather than treadles that are foot operated.

Right in front of the harnesses is a beater with a reed in it. The beater is the swinging arm that is brought forward to push the weft into place after you throw the shot of weft through the shed. In this swinging arm (the beater) is a comb-like device called a reed. The reed has evenly spaced teeth at so many per inch, and its purpose is to hold the warp ends at this spacing. When the beater is used to push the weft into place, it is actually the reed that pushes forward against the cloth.

Just in front of the beater is where the shuttle of weft yarn passes through, where the actual weaving takes place.

The cloth builds up, then, between the beater and the front beam. The purpose of the front beam is to hold the warp at the proper level for the harnesses to work.

Below the front beam is the cloth beam, a rotating beam to hold the woven cloth. It also has a ratchet arrangement, like the warp beam, so that it is held stationary most of the time but you can rotate it when you need to.

So you can see that the basic operation of this loom is like the rigid heddle loom. It looks different, but the major change is that there are more possibilities for threading. Now let's look at how to handle that additional complexity.

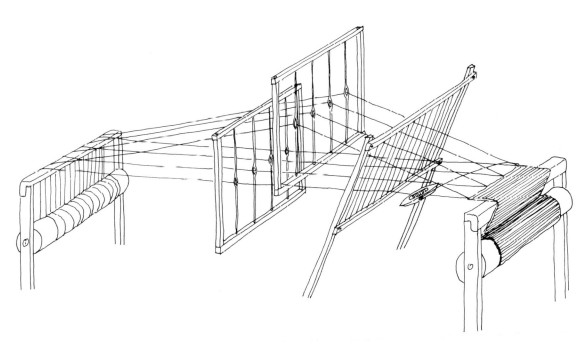

This exaggerated view of a harness loom (with only two harnesses) shows its basic operation.

Drafting

You can see that drafting these more complex patterns will be a little harder than the drafts we looked at for a rigid heddle loom. There the main thing the draft told us was color or yarn type order, since plain weave was the only threading and treadling possibility. But with a harness loom, we can vary the threading, putting any thread on any harness. And if we're working on a floor loom rather than a table model, we can vary the **tie up**, or which harnesses gets connected to which treadle. Then we can vary the **treadling**, or the order that we press these treadles to make the shed. That means the draft has to carry all this information.

No problem. A draft is so organized it makes all this look easy, and you already know the rudiments of draft reading. Let's look at this draft for a 4-harness twill fabric. Weaves have names, some of them descriptive (the generic names) and some of them popular (the brand names). Four-harness twill is a generic name that describes the weave type (twill) and the limits of this one (4-harness).

		X		X	X		X
	X		X	X		X	
	X		X	X			X
X			X		X	X	
					/		
				/			
			/				
	/						

The threading draft is the horizontal bar of squares, as we learned before. Each thread is represented by a column of squares in this bar. Since there are four harnesses on which a warp end could be threaded, each end gets a stack of four squares, with an x to tell which harness it is actually threaded on. So the first thread on the left in this draft is threaded on harness 1. The second thread is on harness 2, the third on 3, and the fourth on 4.

In the corner where the threading draft meets the treadling draft we find the tie-up draft. On a rigid heddle loom there were only two possibilities. We could lift the slots or we could lift the eyes. On a four harness loom there are six possible combinations of two harness lifts, or more possibilities if we want to lift one harness at a time or three at a time. The tie-up draft doesn't show all possible combinations, it only shows those combinations that this weave will actually use. So here we have six combinations in the tie-up draft, or in other words we will tie up six treadles. The first treadle on the left will be attached to harnesses 1 and 2. The second treadle will connect with harness 2 and 3, etc.

Below the tie up draft is the treadling draft. This shows the sequence of harness lifts we will use to put our weft shots through the shed. Since we already have the correct pattern of harnesses fastened to the treadles, we only need to worry about pressing the correct treadle (or operating the correct levers on a table loom). Reading from the bottom up, the first shot of weft is done with treadle 1 pressed. On a table loom, use the levers that lift harnesses 1 and 2. The second shot of weft uses treadle 2, etc. The tie up is usually done so that the treadles are pressed in order if possible, or at least in a sensible, organized pattern if not in straight order.

The draft could also have different symbols for different yarn types or different colors like we saw in the upholstery fabric and the jacket fabric drafts for the rigid heddle loom, rather than the common x. Sometimes the draft will look more complicated because the x's are not in a nice straight line as in this draft, but it's all pretty simple and straightforward really. Just take one section of the draft at a time and follow directions.

Threading the four-harness loom

Let's thread this loom for your next project, three winter scarves in a soft alpaca yarn. See page 79 for yarn requirements.

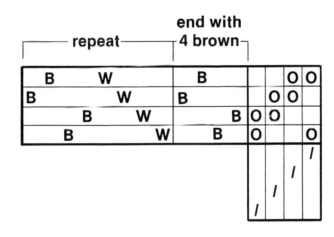

This is the draft for a broken reversed twill, or Dornik twill. Groups of four brown threads alternate with groups of four white threads across the warp.

This weave is popularly called Dornik twill. If you like descriptive names better, it is a broken reverse twill. Broken means that there is a skip in the sequence of threading, where it goes from harness 2 to harness 4. Reverse means that it changes directions in the threading, going from counting up (3-4-1-2) to counting down (4-3-2-1). Twill is the basic weave structure. You can see it is basically like the twill you saw in the drafting lesson.

The draft shows that you need a 4-brown, 4-white color order across the warp, and the written directions say you need 10 e.p.i. for a 7½" width, or a total of 76 warp ends. To start and end this color alternation with brown, you will need 40 ends of brown and 36 ends of white. So wind these two separate 5-yard warps.

Threading the floor or table loom is not too different from threading the rigid heddle loom. Take your predominant color warp (brown in this case) to the loom. Make a tie of the whole warp chain around the front beam, with the cross end long enough to get to the back beam. This knot gives you a firm anchor to pull against when you pull each end through the heddles and tie on in back.

Check the beater to be sure you have the correct size reed there. Reed sizes are expressed in terms of **dents**, the French word for tooth. If there are ten teeth in an inch of the reed, there are also ten spaces. So a 10-dent reed gives ten ends per inch in the warp if every space gets one warp end. Reeds usually have a number stamped into the metal at one end to tell which dent this reed is. If you can't find a number, just measure an inch of the reed and count the spaces. You will need a 10-dent reed for this project.

In order to make room for your hand behind the beater, it is a good idea to tie the beater into an upright position. Make this tie at the left side of the beater if you are right handed, so it is out of your way as you **sley** (thread) the reed.

To sley the reed, I prefer to use a reed hook. This is a flat metal hook with a smoothly rounded, fairly large end. (You can use a crochet hook or just poke each thread through by hand if you prefer.) Now put the cross on your left hand as you did for the rigid heddle loom, and put your right hand with the reed hook behind the beater. Starting at the correct place at the right side to make the scarf be centered (3¾" to the right of center), pull each end through the reed just as you did for the rigid heddle loom.

To thread the heddles, go to the back of the loom. From the back, you thread right to left. Call the harness closest to the front harness #1, which corresponds to the lowest row of squares on the graph paper. So when your draft is laid on a table beside the loom, with the bottom of the draft toward the front of the loom as if the draft were a map of the loom, you will be looking at the threading draft upside down and backwards. Starting at your right on the threading draft, put the threads through the heddles in the order shown.

Threading drafts can always be broken down into units, either a repeat (in this case 3412 1234 is one repeat) or a block. It reduces threading errors if you thread in these groups and check for errors after each group, rather than thread all the way across and then check for

Reed hook

errors. Push all the empty heddles to your left, and then slide back two heddles on each harness. This is one repeat of this threading—3412 1234 will take two heddles on each of the four harnesses. Now starting at your right, pick up the first 8 warp ends from the reed and comb them with your fingers. Put your left hand around these eight heddles and catch the first eight ends between the fingers of your left hand. With your right hand, pick up the first end, pull it towards you, and make a loop near the end. Put this loop through the heddle eye called for in the first square of your draft and, with one smooth motion, push that threaded heddle to the right out of the way. In the same way, pick up the next end and thread it through the next heddle called for on the threading draft.

When you have completed this cluster of eight heddles and eight ends, you will notice if you ended up with an extra heddle or an extra end, or if you ended up with the wrong heddle available. If so, you know you made an error in those eight ends, and you should look for it right now and correct it. If you came out all right on completing those eight ends, you probably did it right and you can go on to the next group without careful rechecking.

When you have threaded the heddles all the way across, you are ready to tie the warp to the warp beam. The warp beam will be fitted with a **tie-on bar**, which is attached to the warp beam with strings or straps or a cloth apron. It is this bar that you will actually tie knots around.

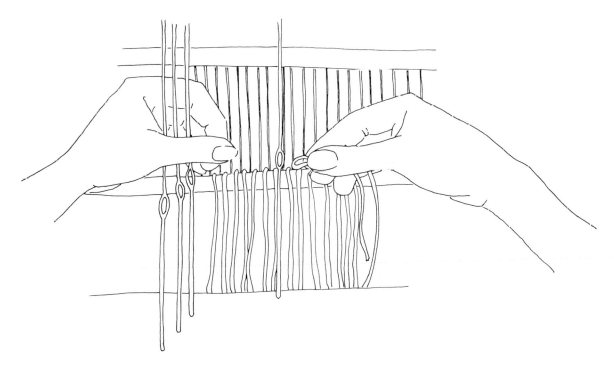

After the warp is threaded through the reed, each thread goes through a heddle.

It is very important that the warp goes *over* the back beam before it does down to the warp beam, in order for the warp to be held at the correct height for the harnesses to work. So at this point release the brake and pull the tie-on bar up over the back beam. Look to be sure that when you turn the warp beam, the warp yarn will be pulled *over* the back beam, not diagonally down from the heddles to the warp beam.

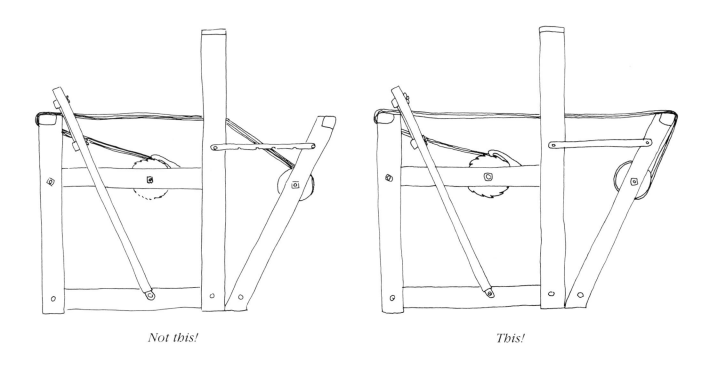

Not this!   *This!*

*Be sure the warp goes over the
back beam before winding it onto
the warp beam.*

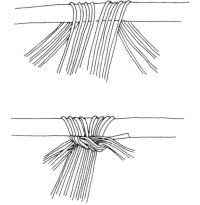

*Here's one way to tie groups of
warp ends onto the apron rod.*

Starting at approximately the center of the warp, pick up a cluster of warp ends about two inches wide or so. Comb this cluster with your fingers as you pull it straight back. Separate the cluster into approximately half, and put the yarn over the bar and then around and up with half the ends coming up on the right and half on the left. Bring these two sets of ends up and tie a square knot above the main cluster of warp ends. Tie the next 2″ section to the left, then the next section to the right. Alternate in this way until all the warp is tied on to the tie on bar.

Now you are ready to wind the warp onto the warp beam. It is basically the same procedure as winding onto the rigid heddle loom. You alternate combing a section with your fingers, dropping it, and turning the warp beam to wind on that section. Pull evenly and firmly on the warp as you then comb out the next section.

Be sure to wind cardboard or heavy paper between layers of the warp.

If you have a somewhat sticky warp, or a fairly closely sett warp, you may find you have less trouble with knots and breakage if you prop open a plain weave shed before you begin to wind on. This helps you separate every other end. If you do prop open the shed, undo your prop when the warp ends approach the reed.

When the end of the warp is even with the front beam, it is time to stop winding the warp and go to tying the warp to the cloth beam tie on bar. Bring the front tie-on bar up over the front beam just as you brought the back one over the back beam before.

Tying on in front is basically the same as tying on in back, with a couple of small exceptions. Once again you start in the approximate center, but this time take clusters of yarn about 1″ wide. These smaller clusters will be easier to even out when you weave the header. Comb this cluster and separate it in half to tie on, but this time tie only the first half of the square knot. The purpose of this step is to get even tension on each thread within the single cluster of yarns, so comb with that in mind. Later you will come back to tie the second half of every square knot while you even up the tension between one cluster and the next. Work from the center outward in each direction, tying the first half of the square knot and concentrating on getting even tension on each end within that single cluster.

When you have done that across the entire warp, you can go back to do the second half of each knot. The purpose in this step is to make each cluster exactly as tight as all previously tied clusters. So start again in the approximate center. Pull up hard on the ends of the knot, and pull to tighten the knot in this position. Complete the square knot. Take the ends of the next cluster and again pull up and tighten the knot. Now feel this cluster and the one you just tied, patting your hand across the tops of the warp. Do the two clusters feel equally tight? If so, tie the second half of the square knot in this cluster. Then tighten the next cluster and feel for even tension before you complete the square knot. Always check the current cluster against all previously tied warp, so the whole thing remains even. Just as you did with the rigid heddle loom, always begin with the center section and work to the right and left.

As you work across the warp, you will find that you need to pull less and less in order to get even tension, because the slack is progressively being pulled out of the warp. That's okay. It is evenness in the finished warp you're after, not evenness of effort in pulling knots.

That's all there is to **dressing the loom**.

Tie-up

On a rigid heddle loom, you would be able to simply start weaving at this piont. That's true, too, if you have a table loom or a floor loom with a **direct tie-up** where each harness is permanently fastened to one treadle. But there are many more possibilities here for raising combinations of harnesses, and many floor looms are made so that you can tie different combinations of harnesses to each treadle. The tie-up draft will tell you what pattern is called for. Remember that the tie-up draft is in the corner, where the threading draft meets the treadling draft. The draft for this project has x's in the first column on the left for harnesses 1 and 2. If you have a table loom or direct tie-up loom, whenever the treadling draft has a mark in that column, you would either depress the levers for those harnesses (on a table loom), or use both feet to depress the treadles for those harnesses (on a direct tie-up floor loom). On a harness loom, tie the first treadle on the left to those two harnesses. The second treadle will be tied to harnesses 2 and 3, and so on. Treadles 5 and 6 are set up to do plain weave. You will use them for weaving the heading. So do the whole tie-up at this point.

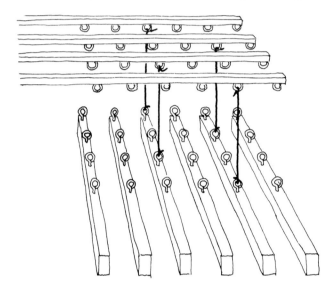

Now weave the heading, lifting harness 1-3 and 2-4 alternately, and check for threading errors and uneven tension in the same way you did before.

That was a fair amount of work, but not as hard as it looked before, don't you think?

Three Soft Winter Scarves

The soft, sophisticated-looking scarves on the next page are all woven on the same warp, one after the other. The changes in pattern that make each one unique are done by changing the weft color order and the treadling. You can make one for yourself and two for gifts.

You already have the loom ready to go and the header woven. Wind a bobbin of white and a bobbin of brown for your boat shuttles (or wind two stick shuttles). Note that the treadling draft on the next page shows scarf A, scarf B, and scarf C. For the first scarf, treadle according to the directions in the A section only, doing the repeats as specified.

WHAT YOU'LL NEED:

EQUIPMENT:

4-harness loom, at least 10″ wide, threaded as described in the previous chapter.
2 shuttles.
Large-eyed tapestry needle.
Cardboard piece, 5″ × 8½″.

MATERIALS:

Warp and weft: wool yarn, about 1800 yd/lb, 6 oz brown and 3 oz white. We used an alpaca yarn from Plymouth Yarns called Indiecita, colors #206 and #201. Sport-weight knitting worsted could be used, too.

PROJECT SPECIFICATIONS:

Warp: 10 e.p.i. × 7½″ wide = 76 ends, 5 yd. long.
Technique: Dornick twill (4-harness reverse broken twill).
Finished Size: 3 scarves each 7″ × 52″.

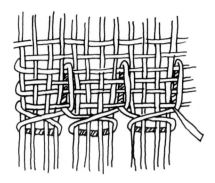

Hemstitch groups of warp ends for a neat, secure fringe.

Begin the first scarf with a left to right shot, leaving a tail of weft yarn at least three times as long as the width of the warp. Weave the first color section of scarf A. Put down your shuttle for now and go back to that long tail of weft you left hanging. Thread it onto a yarn needle to hemstitch the end of the scarf. Here's a version of hemstitching that makes a very tidy, attractive end that is both decorative and functional, as it prevents raveling. Starting at the left edge, put the needle between the fourth and fifth warp ends just below where the weaving starts, and up at the edge. Next, take a vertical stitch, like the blanket stitch shown on page 68, around the first four weft shots, at the point where the fringe clusters separate. Continue across, stitching a cluster of four fringe threads followed by a blanket stitch into the fabric. When you have hemstitched all the way across, push the needle back through the Xs of the hemstitching to secure the end and cut the tail of yarn.

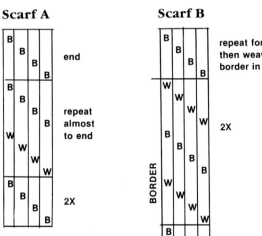

Scarf A

end

repeat almost to end

2X

Scarf B

BORDER

repeat for 46", then weave the border in reverse

2X

3X

Scarf C

repeat for entire length

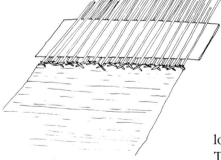

Use a piece of light cardboard between scarves to allow for a fringe when you have finished weaving.

Hemstitch the other end of the scarf, too, after you weave it.

When the entire scarf is finished, including hemstitching on the loom, leave 5″ of unwoven warp before the beginning of the next scarf. The easiest way I know to do this is to cut a 5″ × 8½″ piece of light cardboard, open any shed, and put the cardboard in. Then go on to begin weaving the next scarf, beating the first shot against the cardboard. When you have woven the first section of the next scarf, remove the cardboard and hemstitch the end. Use the same cardboard again to separate the second and third scarves.

The versatile brown-and-white striped warp is treadled three different ways for these soft scarves.

You will need to be very careful to beat this fabric very lightly, just hard enough to square the fabric. You are trying for a balanced weave, where the warp and weft show equally in the finished fabric. So every four weft shots should make a perfectly square design with a four-thread colored section of the warp. If you beat too hard, you will get a weft-predominant fabric that not only looks bad because the pattern doesn't show well, but also feels bad because it is too stiff for a scarf.

When you have finished weaving and hemstitching the third scarf, cut or untie the fabric from the loom, being sure to leave more than 2½″ of warp at each end for the fringe. Handwash the entire length of three scarves in warm water with a handwash detergent like Woolite®. Dry flat and steam press lightly when almost dry. Then cut the beginning and ending fringes to 2½″ and cut between the scarves. Cutting after washing instead of before reduces the tangling of the fringe. Did you notice how the beginning and ending fringes tried to tangle, but the fringes between scarves didn't? I believe in doing things the easy way!

Here you used one warp to make three unique items. You saw a glimpse of this trick earlier when you wove a sample of ribbed fabric at the end of the upholstery fabric project. You could have easily threaded the warp twice as long for that project and made two chair seats in co-ordinated fabrics. That's a good thing to keep in mind any time you plan a project. Threading the loom is the most tedious part of weaving, so getting two or more different items from one warp is always a treat.

The Sweater Look
In An Overshot Weave

Warmth and beauty—what more could you ask? Jean Scorgie designed a handwoven interpretation of a Fair Isle sweater, which is shown on the next page.

WHAT YOU'LL NEED:

EQUIPMENT:
4-harness loom, at least 24″ wide.
12-dent reed.
7 shuttles.
2 #1 knitting needles, 14″ long.
Sewing machine (optional).

MATERIALS:
1 lb. of wool yarn, about 2000 yd/lb. We used a singles from Harrisville Yarns, color oatmeal.
1 433-yd skein each of 6 different colors of pattern wool, about 1790 yd/lb. We used a Finnish wool called Helmi Vuorelma Oy Vippela from Schoolhouse or Eaton Yarns in cerise #108, red #109, orange #110, rust #112, green #115, and brown ÷124.
Notions: 3 ⁷⁄₁₆″ buttons, matching thread.

PROJECT SPECIFICATIONS:
Warp: 12 e.p.i. × 24″ width = 290 ends, 3 ⅓ yd long.
Technique: Overshot weave and knit trim.
Finished Fabric Size: 22″ × 2 yd 6″ for a woman's medium.

Our colonial ancestors made coverlets of this weave, known as overshot. Though derived from European sources, overshot was so refined here, and was redesigned and woven so many times, that it can be said to be the first (perhaps the only) truly American weave. What I find interesting, though, is the adaptation Jean has made to another use. Colonial weavers certainly never used this weave for clothing—they had linsey-woolsey and other fabrics for that. But most any weave can be adapted for most any use. The restrictions depend more on how long the floats are or other practical considerations like that than on what use someone else had for that weave. I have Peter Collingwood's book *The Techniques of Rug Weaving* not because I like to weave rugs (which I don't) but because it has interesting weaves. I've used many of them for clothing, just changing the yarn size, tightness of beat, etc. to make the cloth lighter and more flexible. So in your further exploration of weaving, look in every book that interests you and be willing to reinterpret.

Notice how this threading draft looks more complicated? The Xs don't just march up and down in diagonal rows. But they do have a tidy order to them. Note how there are blocks that work on two harnesses. There is a block that uses harnesses 1 and 2. Beside it there is a block that uses harnesses 2 and 3. When you look at the sweater, you can see that the pattern consists of blocks, too. So when you thread the heddles, those blocks are the units that you use for counting out the heddles and self-checking the threading.

Threading																			H1	H2	H3	H4		
X	X																X	X			O O		O	O
	X				X	X	X		X	X	X							X		O O		O		O
X			X	X	X	X	X	X	X	X	X	X	X					X	O O			O		O
	X	X	X	X				X				X	X	X	X	X	X		O		O O		

Treadling (USE TABBY):

	H1	H2	H3	H4	H5
6X				1	1
green	2	1	1		
orange / red / rust / red / orange (A)					
red / cerise / rust / cerise / red (B)		6 / 6 / 6	6 / 2 / 6		
green	2	1	1		
6X				1	1
rust	1	1			
brown		1	2 / 1		
rust	1	1			
tabby 6X				1	1

This draft also has something new in the treadling draft. Note how it says "use tabby" along the edge. This tells you about half the threads in the entire weft! Tabby is another name for plain weave when it's used as a stabilizing background in pattern weaves. This sweater has oatmeal-colored plain weave background with a design in shades of red. To weave this tabby ground, you must put a plain weave shot between each pattern shot. So "use tabby" always means weave one shot of background weft on the odd harnesses, weave one pattern shot, weave one shot of background weft on the even harnesses, and then weave the next pattern shot. Continue to alternate the two plain weave treadles with each pattern shot in turn.

With all that expressed in the two words "use tabby", then all the treadling draft needs to tell you is what order to do pattern shots. That is quite a bit to tell you, actually, as you can see by the complexity of the treadling draft. This treadling has two things you haven't seen before. It has notes with an ×, like 6×, in the margin, and it has numbers in the little squares with color names beside.

"6×" in the margin means do this 6 times. So where you treadle plain weave (the last two treadles) in oatmeal background yarn, you repeat that two shot sequence 6 times for a total of 12 shots before going on to the next instruction. Note that overshot is a balanced plain weave, so be sure you are getting 12 picks per inch to match your 12 e.p.i. warp.

Where the draft gives a number in the square, that means use this treadle this many times. Since there is a tabby shot between these repeats of the same treadle, it won't just unweave. Repeating the same treadle 6 times is how you build up those blocks of solid color in shades of red to make the flowers in the pattern. The draft also names colors for each section or, in the flower blocks, beside each treadling instruction. So to weave flower A, you do 6 shots on treadle 4 with orange (with tabby shots between), then 6 shots on treadle 3 with red yarn, then 2 shots on treadle 4 with rust yarn, etc. You'll need quite a few shuttles, but otherwise it's not hard.

That's all you need to know in general about reading this draft, so let's go on now to the specifics of this project.

Go through the draft from the bottom up. To make the colors match at the side seam, weave block A, then B A B B A B A. The two B's will be separated by the fold at the shoulder.

When you have finished weaving, make the hand-knit bands. For each wristband, cast on 70 stitches, using #1 straight needles, 14" long. Knit 1, purl 1 until the piece measures 2½" wide. Bind off and use the tail of the yarn to sew the two ends together into a circle.

For the waistband, use the same ribbing technique for 240 stitches by 2".

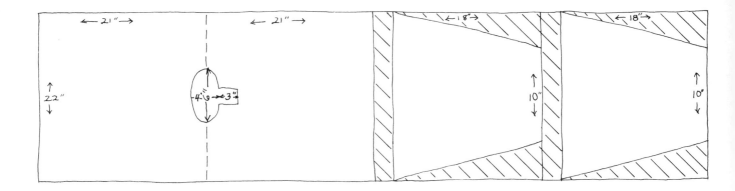

The neckband is a little more complex. Cast on 220 sts. The mitered corners at each side will be formed by decreasing 3 sts down to 1 st every even-numbered row. Row 1 (and all odd-numbered rows except row 5): k1, p1, repeat to the end of the row. Row 2: (k1, p1) 19 times, sl 1, k2 tog, psso, (p1, k1) 69 times, sl 1, k2 tog, psso, (k1, p1) 19 times. Row 3: same as row 1. Row 4: knit as row 2, centering the decreases above the previous ones. Row 5 (buttonhole row): k1, ★ (p1, k1) 5 times, yo, k2 tog (buttonhole formed), repeat from ★ 2 times, p1, k1 to the end of the row. Continue decreasing for the mitered corners on the even-numbered rows and knitting plain on the odd rows until there are 14 rows. Bind off.

Wash the fabric and knit trim, dry flat, and press well. Cut out the pieces and straight-stitch the neck and sleeve edges, zigzag stitch the waistline cut edges. Attach the neckband by sewing, right sides together, with a ¼ " seam that covers the straight stitching you did around the neck. Be sure the buttonholes are on the right before you sew. Then turn the seam back toward the body of the sweater and trim the woven fabric if necessary so that the edge of the ribbing covers the raw edge of the woven fabric on the inside of the neck. Sew the edge of the ribbing down ¼ " in from the ribbing seam with decorative topstitching. Sew buttons on left side, matching buttonholes.

Attach the sleeves and sew the side seams. Attach the wristbands and the waist ribbing in the same way as you did the neckline ribbing, and you're done.

"Overshot" was favored by our Colonial ancestors for blankets, and it's still exciting today for clothing, table linens and wall hangings.

"Summer and Winter" is the old-time name for this weave, which was often used in Colonial coverlets. The reverse side is just the opposite in color.

A Block Weave Rug

This handsome rug was designed by Jean Anstine. It has a warm, traditional look in the natural wools Jean has selected, but would also lend itself well to bold, contemporary color schemes.

Like the sweater we just finished, this is a block weave project. That's pretty obvious from just looking at the rug. The color areas occur in blocks. In this case the weave is called "summer & winter" weave. The back of the rug is just like the front, only the colors are reversed. This would be a great weave structure to play with on your own, without needing to look up anything in a book, because just rearranging the two blocks can lead to a variety of unique designs.

WHAT YOU'LL NEED:

EQUIPMENT:
- 4-harness floor loom, at least 36″ wide.
- 5- or 10-dent reed.
- 2 rug or stick shuttles.

MATERIALS:
Warp: 12 oz of 8/4 linen rug warp, or strong cotton twine at about 500 yd/lb.
Weft: Rug wool at about 288 yd/lb. Jean used 6-ply rug wool from Wilde Yarns in fawn and brown, about 2½ lb of each color.

PROJECT SPECIFICATIONS:
Warp: 5 e.p.i. × 36″ wide = 180 ends plus 2 floating selvedges 2 yd long.
Technique: Weft-face summer & winter woven on opposites.

Because this weave structure is so simple and orderly, we don't even need a full draft of the threading. We can work from a profile draft. The profile draft is not only easier to write, it is also more like a picture of the finished product. It makes it easier to visualize the finished effect, and it makes it easier to see if your proportions look good just from looking at the draft.

Summer & winter weave on four harnesses can have two blocks. We'll call these blocks Block A and Block B. Within Block A, the threading goes 1-3-2-3. This four-end sequence is repeated for as wide as you want Block A to be. So the total width of Block A can be any multiple of four warp ends. Block B, on the other hand, is threaded 1-4-2-4. Repeat this four-end sequence for as wide as you want Block B to be.

Now to make our draft, we have only to indicate how wide Block A will be and how wide Block B will be. We could express this in inches, I suppose, but threading drafts deal with ends, not inches. So we express the width of each block in terms of repeats of the four-end basic threading unit. The profile draft looks like this:

The lower row of squares in the threading draft represents Block A, and the upper row represents Block B. Each square across represents a four-end repeat. So we begin with six repeats of the Block A threading, or in other words a 24-end width of color in our rug. This will be one of the dark corner blocks. Then we have four repeats of the Block B threading, making that area 16 ends wide in total, and so on.

Can you see how the profile draft is like a graphic representation of the look of the finished rug? It gives a visual feel for the proportions of the brown versus the fawn. It is easier to picture this rug at a glance than to picture the sweater from a glance at its draft.

Wind on the warp carefully, getting the tension absolutely even and pulling the slack out of the warp as you wind on. Linen is the most difficult warp because it has no stretch, so if you're using it, the tension must be *very* even. If you use a 10-dent reed, thread one warp end through every other dent to get 5 e.p.i.

A word here about the **floating selvedges** mentioned in the project specifications. These are the warp ends at each edge. Thread them through the reed along with all the rest of the ends, but not through any heddle. They will stay in a "neutral" position as you weave, and help you keep neat edges on your rug. Always put your shuttle *over* the floating selvedge as it enters the shed, and take it out *under* the floating selvedge on the other side. Floating selvedges are useful for lots of different kinds of weaves where weft tends not to catch the edge thread on every shot.

Leave about 12″ for fringe (you can include the tie-on knots in this). Weave using your dark and light shuttles alternately, and treadle 1-2-3-4 just as the treadling draft tells you.

A		B		1	2	3	4
		4	4	O		O	
3	3				O		O
2		2		O	O		
1		1				O	O
							D
						L	
	II				D		
				L			
							L
						D	
	I				L		
				D			

Note that the treadling order is always this four-treadle repeat, regardless of what order the colors are going. As you weave, lay the first shuttle in the repeat close to you on your loom bench, and the next shuttle farther away. You need a set plan like this for handling the shuttles to make the color changes look good at the selvedges.

Weave using your shuttles alternately as follows:

   Dark-light (block I) — 5¼″
   Light-dark (block II)— 3¼″
   Dark-light (block I) — 1½″
   Light-dark (block II)—40″
   Dark-light (block I) — 1½″
   Light-dark (block II)— 3¼″
   Dark-light (block I) — 5¼″

When the rug is woven, work a Damascus edge all the way across so that the ends of the rug will be firmly secured.

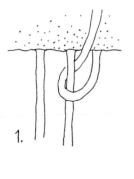

1.

2.

With the edge of the rug facing you, work from right to left, looping each warp end around its neighbor. Your fringe will now be lying on top of the rug.

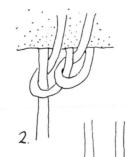

3.

4.

Start at the right edge again and work back across so the fringe is hanging down again. You can leave the fringe like this (it will ravel some with use), or braid it as shown on the next page.

Then take groups of four warp ends and work four-strand braids all the way across. Secure the end of each braid by wrapping one of the warps around it and knotting it. Trim the braids evenly.

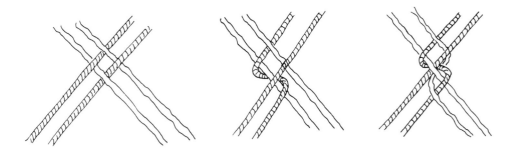

Don't be alarmed if your finished rug looks a little lumpy or uneven at this point. Roll it in a wet sheet for several hours, then lay it out flat to dry. You can steam press it if necessary.

Trouble Shooting

There are a few issues that come up in most any project, no matter how expert and experienced you are. Here are some of the problems and what to do about them:

Broken warp end: It's quite common for a warp end to break as you are weaving, or for a knot in the warp to show up. The broken piece of yarn that is attached to the web should be brought forward and pinned to the cloth, out of the way. Then make a butterfly of extra warp yarn (see page 29) for how to make a butterfly). With the beginning end of the butterfly, the part that was hanging down to your elbow when you started making it, go to the back of the loom and thread the heddle that was left empty by the broken warp. Pull the back half of the broken piece of warp out of the way so it is hanging from the warp beam. That keeps it from tangling the other warp ends as you weave. Now thread your replacement warp end through the empty spot in the reed. Pin the end of this new warp to your fabric in the right spot, using a large pin and figure-eighting the yarn around it. At the back pull out the butterfly until it hangs half way between the back beam and the floor. Make a slip knot in this new replacement warp so that, when you pull, the end toward the heddles is the end that slips through. In this slip knot loop, fasten a weight of some kind. I use duck decoy weights from the local hunter's store, but any piece of weaving or kitchen equipment will do. The object is to put this new warp end under tension, like the other warp ends, without having to wind it around the warp beam. With your new weighted replacement warp end, you are ready to weave on.

When you have woven far enough that the original warp end will reach forward past the front edge of the woven cloth, it is time to thread the broken end through the heddle (doubled up with the replacement end that is already there) and forward through the reed. Pin it to the cloth as you did before. Now weave 2″ with both the original end and the replacement end weaving in the same spot. After 2″, cut out the replacement end, cutting right at the front edge of the woven cloth. You will not need to go back and work on this spot with a needle later because you have already overlapped the two warps by 2″ of weaving.

When you take the finished fabric off the loom, you will need to go in with a yarn needle and repair the place where the replacement warp

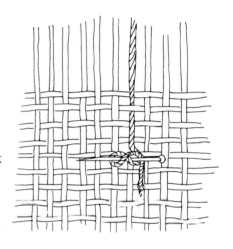

Mend a broken warp by pinning a new one to the woven cloth and hanging it off the back of the loom with a weight on the end.

end began. Weave one end in with the needle so that the two warp ends overlap by about 2″, just as a new weft thread begins by overlapping the old weft about 2″.

Knot in the warp: If you see a knot in the warp coming before the reed makes it break, you can make an easier job of repairing it than if you just wait till it breaks. Some knots are so small that you can weave right over them, and then go in with a needle after the cloth is off the loom to add a replacement thread that starts 2″ before the knot and weaves along till 2″ after the knot. Then just cut out the knot.

If the knot will be too big to go through the reed many times without breaking, add a replacement warp before the knot gets to the reed. Weave with both the knotted warp and the replacement warp for 2″ or so, then cut out the knotted warp and pull it to the back out of the way. When you have woven a few inches, you can bring the original warp, with the knot cut out, back through the heddle and the reed as described above for a broken warp end. Doing it this way makes it possible to do no needle repair after the cloth is off the loom.

Weft is not straight: If you weave your cloth and see that the weft doesn't remain straight after you beat it into place, your problem is uneven tension. Where the weft mounds up toward the reed, you have looser tension. Where it dips down toward the front beam, the tension is tighter. If you see this at the very beginning, when you are weaving the header, you can fix it by retying the warp to the bar of the cloth beam. But if the problem shows up after you have woven several inches, you need to fix the problem from the back of the loom. And you need to remember to be more careful to get even tension next time you wind on your warp.

First look carefully to see where the tension is looser—where the weft lumps up toward the reed. Then at the back of the loom you can either tie a weight to that section of warp and hang the weight down below the warp beam, or you can stuff a pencil, folded paper, or what have you between the warp beam and the offending section of warp. The object here is to pull on that loose section of warp until it is as tight as the rest of the warp. You can tell when you have it right by beating your cloth once more and watching to see if the weft stays straight. If it does, you have even tension.

If you have fixed the problem by stuffing something between the warp beam and the loose warp, you will have to put the object back in place every time you wind the warp forward. But that is better than ending up with a lumpy or curved finished product. In my early days as a weaver, I wove a project in which the left side was slightly looser than the right throughout the whole weaving process. But since the weft went straight, just slanting up toward the left, I decided not to fix it with weights. When I took the finished table runner off the loom, the whole thing curved—I had a C-shaped runner! It's better to fix this problem as you weave than to have a ridiculous looking finished product.

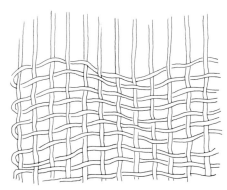

If your weft is wavy after beating, it probably means that your tension isn't even.

Starting a new weft thread: To start a new piece of weft when your shuttle runs out of thread, just overlap the new thread with the old for about 2″. Unless you have some special reason, this can happen anywhere across the width of the warp. In fact, it's better if it happens in different places each time so there is no buildup from having doubled weft in the same spot repeatedly.

If you are doing weft stripes, your new weft starts pretty much have to all come at the edge. If the project will have seams along the edges, make your overlaps short enough to be hidden by the seams. If the weft is bulky enough to cause a noticeable lump, try working in the ending weft piece by carrying it along the selvedge, catching it with every turn of the weft yarn, for an inch or two. If you are doing a plaid, the changes of weft color are least conspicuous if you make your overlap in the section of warp that matches your new weft color. This is actually less noticeable than starting the new color at the selvedge.

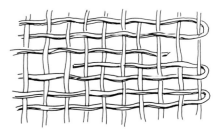

Start a new weft by overlapping the end of the old one a little.

Weaving with two colors (carrying one along): When you are weaving horizontal stripes, changing back and forth between two colors, it is better to carry the other color along than to have the extra buildup caused by overlapping as you start and stop each color. Just loop the working weft around the resting weft at each turn around the edge, as the illustration shows.

Threading error: When you weave the header, check carefully for threading errors. Sometimes you will find that you mixed up the order, threading 1 3 2 4 when you meant to thread 1 2 3 4, for example. In this case, it will be easy to untie one knot at the cloth beam rod, rethread the mixed-up threads in the right order through the heddles and the reed, and then retie the knot.

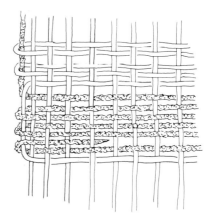

Carry one weft color up the side until you need it again when weaving weft stripes.

Missing warp end: Another threading error may be that you completely missed a thread in your pattern. In this case, you just need to add an extra warp end as you would add one to repair a broken warp end. Be sure your butterfly has yarn at least as long as your entire warp, as it will need to be carried that long. You may have to rethread the reed to allow space for this new end if you only missed it in the heddles but not in the reed. If so, look first to see which direction is closest to the edge, and re-sley the reed in that direction.

Extra warp end or **Incorrect sleying of the reed:** Sometimes you accidentally put two ends through the same dent of the reed. You will need to re-sley the reed from the place of the mistake to the nearer edge of the warp.

Breaking selvedge threads: This is caused by too much pull-in, so that the reed rubs too hard on the edge threads each time you beat. Put more slack in your weft yarn on each shot. The problem is worse on weft-face fabrics, as there the weft must take a very serpentine path while the warp stays quite straight.

Fabric getting narrower as you weave: This is really the same problem as breaking selvedge threads, just an earlier stage. So try the same solution—more slack in your weft.

Warp fraying and breaking: If this happens in some place other than the selvedge, it probably means your reed is too fine so it's rubbing the yarn to shreds. Re-sley looser in another reed, or double the ends in a reed with half as many teeth per inch. This will give you the same number of ends per inch but with less wear on the yarn. If the threads are fraying only at the selvedge, see **Breaking selvedge threads** above.

Can't beat weft in tightly enough: Your sett is too tight. Either re-sley to fewer ends per inch or use a thinner weft thread.

Weft packing in too tightly: Your sett is too loose. Either re-sley to more ends per inch, or use a fatter weft thread.

Can't get a shed to open: There are various possible explanations for this, but by far the most likely is that you forgot to go over the back beam before you tied on to the warp beam rod. Many looms have a removeable back beam, so you can remove it, slip it under the warp between the heddles and the cloth beam, and raise it (and the warp with it) back into place. Then the warp will be travelling from the heddles, over the back beam, down to the warp beam as it should be.

Removing the finished product from the loom: This is not a problem, this is a triumph! Wind your cloth forward so that a lot of warp is between the reed and the front beam. If your next project is likely to be the same ends per inch with the same threading, you will want to save this threading by putting a long piece of masking tape across the entire warp at the reed. Preserving this threading will make it possible to tie on a new warp, rather than completely rethreading. Then cut the warp between the reed and the edge of the finished cloth, allowing enough length for fringe if that is part of your plan. Unwind the cloth from the cloth beam and cut or untie it there.

Tying on a new warp: If you have left your previous warp on the loom, secured with masking tape at the front of the reed when you cut off your last project, then you can tie on a new warp that is to be the same threading in the same ends per inch and the same width. Just take each end of new warp from the cross and tie it to the next available old warp end, working across the width of the loom. This is simpler than rethreading, though it is some genuine work to tie 300 individual knots.

Planning a Project On Your Own

We've gone through several projects by now with me telling you exactly what to do, though you may have noticed my directions have gotten more and more sketchy as you have learned more and more. You probably feel reasonably confident by now that you can go on from here. You know how to thread three kinds of looms, so you could no doubt transfer that understanding to any loom you might come across. You know a few weaves and how to read a draft, so you could look through other weaving books to find a weave structure you want to try. The only gap in your knowledge now, I think, is in how to put the variables together to plan a project completely on your own. This is something like learning menu planning as the last part of a cooking course. You already know most of what you need, you just need to know how to put it together.

There are two major classifications of things to think about when you plan a weaving project. The first is design considerations, the other is practical considerations. In the design time you ask yourself where you are headed. How to get there is a practical consideration.

Design considerations

Where am I headed? What do I want to accomplish? What do I want to make and what are its inherent requirements? Questions like these begin the design process.

Design sources

Designs can start from several sources, but probably the most common among weavers is designing from function. You want to make some useful object, and your design centers around the requirements of that object.

Let's say, for example, that you want to make a winter hat. Your major purpose then would be to stay warm. Your secondary purpose would be to look good. Perhaps a third would be to coordinate with your winter coat. As soon as the purpose is clear in your mind, you are ready to consider the shape, color, and texture of the hat of your dreams.

I'd always advise starting with the dream. Soon enough we'll get to the reality of what is possible on the loom you have with the yarn that is available. But dreaming about the most wonderful hat imaginable will help you come out with a good hat, and it will help you have fun doing it. And isn't fun what it's all about?

Another common design source is designing from the materials. The first time you walk into a really good yarn store, you'll know what I mean. There will be this absolutely wonderful yarn that you simply can't resist buying. Then you'll get home and think "Now what am I going to do with this?" Your design plan will center around making something that shows off this yarn to the maximum, that really uses whatever qualities attracted you to it in the first place. If it is linen, you'll think of making some table linens—you wouldn't think of making a winter hat. But if it is soft, fuzzy wool, you will think of a hat, never a table linen. So the material governs the design. I call this the yarn store ecstacy, and you haven't lived till you've experienced it!

Many designs come from a strong interest in a particular technique. The window covering we made may well have come from such a source. Perhaps you get interested in all the ways you can make lace-like fabrics. Holes really are fascinating. So then you ask yourself "What can I make that uses lace techniques? What are the possibilities of this technique that I can explore?"

Other designs come from a real visual source. Many tapestries are inspired in this way. If your main purpose is to represent that visual source, abstractly or realistically or whatever, then your choices of shape, color, and texture will be governed by that purpose.

Purpose

Any of these sources is as valuable as any other. They are all good, but they will lead to different design decisions. In any case, the first step in designing is to decide what you want, what your purpose is.

Shape

Next, look at shape, color, and texture with that purpose in mind. What overall shape will accomplish your purpose? If it's a winter hat, you may decide it needs to cover your ears and the top of your head. Does it need to be tied on or otherwise fastened under the chin? Do you want a large and fantastic area on the top of the head, too? What overall shape will suit your purpose and suit your fancy?

Then, what interior shapes will echo and enhance that overall shape? Would a horizontal band around the bottom edge of a ski hat look good with the shape of the hat and the shape of your face? Or is there some way to echo the shape of the overall hat in the smaller colored shapes on the surface of the hat? The interior shapes should, ideally, be related to the overall shape.

Color

Color inspirations can come from a variety of sources. Sometimes your color choices are dictated by a need to coordinate with something else. You may want your handwoven winter hat to look good with your winter coat, and that governs your color decisions.

Other times your color choices will be governed by that yarn store ecstacy. You have this wonderful yarn, and the only color choices left are if you will use other colors with this one.

But more often your dream design is free and open in terms of color choices. So how do you come up with good color combinations? While this is probably the most fun part of weaving, I've always been surprised at how many of my beginning students are timid about choosing colors.

There are many good books available about color theory, where you can learn about value, hue, chroma, and so on. But perhaps the easiest way for a beginner to deal with color is through looking at nature, art, or museum crafts.

If you leaf through a copy of *National Geographic* magazine till you find a photo you like (probably no later than page 2 in this wonderful magazine), you can have a ready-made color scheme. What are the colors in the photo? How much of each color is there, proportionately? If you match both the colors and the relative amounts of each color, you will have a combination you already know is appealing.

The same technique works with observing nature and copying its colors. One of my earliest projects came about from a glimpse of nature. I was in my basement and glanced up out the window. The sky was a beautiful blue, and across the window was a birch branch—white with flecks of brown. I wove a table runner in those colors, with mostly sky blue, less white, and a tiny bit of brown. I was really pleased with the result.

Plain weave in warm, wooly yarns makes a soft fabric that can be cut and sewn into a woven hat. A matching plaid scarf completes the set.

Art, especially art of other cultures, will give you some great color ideas. Looking at Japanese prints is one of my favorite sources when I think my color sense needs a shot in the arm.

Remember that we're talking only about color here. You don't need to weave a picture of a birch branch or imitate the shapes in the *National Geographic* photo. Just copy the colors and the proportions. Your finished product might be a striped hat with the colors of a Van Gogh painting of haystacks. Van Gogh's colors will make your hat beautiful.

Texture

When you have decided on shape and color, you have done the major portion of your design dreaming. But texture is another design element that you can consider at this point. Would smooth or fuzzy fit your purpose better? How about shiny or flat? Different yarns and different weaves can accomplish different degrees of surface texture.

Practical considerations

After you have a clear idea of what you want to make, the next question is how to make it. You need to realize, though, that sometimes there is a give and take between the design and the practicalities. Perhaps the loom won't let you use as fuzzy a yarn as you wanted because it would tangle too much to get the shed open. Or maybe the perfect yarn in your imagination simply doesn't exist. As you plan how to accomplish your dream product, practical considerations nearly always force some shifts in the idea itself.

Choosing the right fiber

There are several practical considerations that need to be taken into account on any woven project, regardless of whether the finished product will be a hat for the winter or a huge wall sculpture. First of all, you need to choose a suitable fiber. Fiber is the raw material of yarn. Cotton, wool, and polyester are all fibers. They have different characteristics, both in their performance in the finished product and in their behavior as you are weaving them.

Which particular qualities you want will depend on what product you wish to make. In making clothing, the drape of the finished product will be important, either to make the fabric crisp enough to tailor or soft enough to make a flowing dress. Moisture absorption and heat conductivity will determine how comfortable it is in the season you intend to wear it. The fabric's washability and tendency to absorb or repel dirt will be important. If you want to make a drapery fabric, you'll want to consider the fiber's resistance to sun damage and its flammability. Woven sculpture usually requires control of the drape or stiffness of the fabric, some consideration of its ability to look clean for a long time, and some thought about its strength.

Whatever your intended product, look at what qualities it demands and what qualities the various possible fiber choices offer. Each fiber has its own natural drape, moisture absorption, heat conductivity, washability, wrinkle resistance, sunlight resistance, and strength.

Weave two shawls from one long warp. This warp shades gradually from royal blue to emerald; one plain weave shawl is woven with blue weft, one with green. Woven by Judy Steinkoenig.

Resilience is the ability of a fiber to stretch and then spring back to its original length. A more resilient fiber is easier to use as warp because it makes up for slight unevenness in your tension. It will stretch a little when you make it too tight, and spring up a bit when you make it a little too loose. It forgives your minor errors. That's why wool or even cotton are easy warps, but linen can be quite a problem. With linen you must get even tension because it won't forgive you a thing.

Drape is important to clothing. Fabric for clothing should have body but not be too stiff.

Wool and silk are particularly satisfying fibers to use when drape is important. Rayon is a little more limp, and cotton is quite limp. For the chioli top we made, this extreme amount of drape was quite appropriate, but it wouldn't have been suitable for the log cabin jacket. Linen, on the other hand, is quite stiff, so a 100% linen handwoven blouse might be unsuccessful. Among the synthetic fibers, orlon, acetate, and some nylons have the best draping qualities. Handwoven polyester fabrics lack body so they are not very satisfying in their drapability.

Moisture absorption and heat conductivity. How well a fiber absorbs moisture and how it conducts heat both have a big influence on how it feels in a clothing fabric. Non-absorbing fabric feels clammy when the weather is too hot, chilling when the temperature goes down. That's why a plastic raincoat is unbearable as soon as the rain stops and the sun comes out. It can't let your body moisture out. Moisture-absorbing fabrics are more comfortable, especially when the temperature, humidity, or activity levels are likely to change.

Heat conductivity is also important in choosing a fiber for clothing fabric. Wool is moisture absorbing but not heat conducting. Moisture absorption makes wool comfortable in a wide variety of temperatures, and its non-conductivity makes it especially comfortable in cold weather when it keeps your body heat in.

Silk is similar to wool in these two characteristics. Silk is often thought of as a summer fabric, but it is cool only when woven as a very thin fabric. In thicker yarns it makes good winter clothing.

Cotton is moisture absorbing and heat conducting, so it is comfortable to wear in a wide variety of conditions. Since it lets your body heat escape, it is especially suited to summer clothing. Linen is also both moisture absorbing and heat conducting.

Man-made fibers are not moisture absorbing. Their heat conductivity depends largely on how they are made. They are not particularly good conductors to begin with but they can be made to capture heat in small air pockets by being crimped during manufacturing, so smooth synthetics are generally cooler than those made to look like wool.

Cleanliness and washability. How readily a fiber attracts and holds dirt and how easily it gives it up in cleaning are important for clothing, interior design fabrics, and for woven art work which will seldom if ever be washed or dry cleaned. Fibers with smooth surfaces, as seen under a microscope, are most dirt resistant since the dirt has fewer places to stick than on a rough-surfaced fiber.

Glass fiber and other synthetics, silk, and linen all have smooth surfaces that resist dust collection. Most of the rayons shed dirt reasonably well. Cotton has a fairly short fiber and a somewhat rough surface, so it holds dust more. Wool, because of its scaly surface, attracts and holds dust.

Wrinkle resistance. In these days of wash-and-wear fabrics and the electric dryer, we all know the value of wrinkle resistance. Does anybody ever use an iron any more?

Wool and its kinfolk—alpaca, camel, mohair, and cashmere—are excellent wrinkle resisters. Silk also resists wrinkles well. Cotton and linen wrinkle easily.

Flammability. Clothing and interior design fabrics need some resistance to fire. There are laws about children's sleepwear and about fabrics for public buildings, but even without a specific law I'd rather be careful. It's not only in love that I don't want to get burned.

The Fort Worth Weaver's Guild all wove guest towels one year, and here are a few results. The yarns are fine cotton and linen, the borders fancy overshots and twills.

All fibers react to strong heat, but some react with a flame and others do not. Acetate, dacron, nylon, and orlon fuse and shrink away from the heat, but they don't flame. Wool and other animal fibers, as well as cotton, linen, and ramie, will burn. The plant fibers such as cotton will burn and continue to smolder after the flame is out, while wool burns less enthusiastically and will not smolder after the flame is out. Wool self-extinguishes. Rayon burns well—that's why it can't be used in children's pajamas.

But besides the fiber content, flammability depends on the tightness of the spin and the weave, on how much air they let in to assist the burning. So a burn test will tell you more concrete information. Flammability of a finished fabric can be tested by holding an edge of the fabric to an open flame for 60 seconds. When you remove it from the flame, time how quickly the flame self-extinguishes. Anything that keeps burning for 30 seconds is dangerous. Many fabrics will self-extinguish faster than you could time—in less than one second.

Resistance to sunlight. Any fabric that will hang in direct sunlight, such as draperies, will need to resist sun rot. Rayon is quite resistant to sun rot, though you might not want to use it as drapery fabric because of its flammability. Next best is linen, then cotton. Among the man-made fibers, glass, polyester, and orlon keep their strength in sunlight, while nylon will deteriorate after long exposure. Silk is the weakest of all in this respect.

Tensile strength and abrasion resistance. The strength of a fiber influences how long the resulting fabric will wear, especially under heavy use. This is especially important for upholstery fabrics and clothing, for straps of all kinds, and for large art pieces where the top must support the weight of the whole work.

Strength has two aspects: tensile strength, which keeps a fiber from tearing under lengthwise stress, and abrasion resistance, which keeps it from wearing away by rubbing. A large fiber artwork will need tensile strength; upholstery fabric will need abrasion resistance.

For tensile strength, fiberglas, nylon and polyester rate very high. Silk is the strongest natural fiber, though it is weaker when it is wet. Linen is very strong, and gets stronger when it is wet. Cotton is quite strong, and it too gets stronger when it is wet, an increase of as much as 30%. Mercerizing makes it even stronger, though still not as strong as silk or linen of the same dry size. Rayon is weaker than cotton when dry, and loses 40% to 70% of its strength when wet. Wool has the lowest tensile strength of the natural fibers, and is even weaker when wet.

Nylon has great resistance to abrasion, which is probably why it is so widely used in upholstery and carpets. Dacron and ramie are strong against abrasion, while cotton, linen, silk and wool are rated only fair.

That's a lot of information, and you can see that a fiber that is good in one of the qualities you need may not be too good in another. There is often a trade-off. To help make all these comparisons clearer, here is a chart that covers those fibers most commonly available to handweavers:

This bag by Connie Farnbach has a warp-face inkle band strap, and weft-predominant body woven with narrow rag strips for weft.

FIBER CHARACTERISTICS

Fiber Type	Resilience	Abrasion Resistance	Drape	Moisture Absorption
Natural				
wool	good	fair	good	good
cotton	good	fair	limp	very good
silk	good	fair	good	good
linen	poor	poor	stiff	good
Reconstructed				
rayon	fair	poor	good	fair
Man-Made				
nylon	fair	good	good	poor

Yarn types

The type of spin given to the fiber is also a practical consideration in your design.

The first step in spinning is to make a **singles** yarn. This is one long cluster of carded or combed fiber that is then twisted. Singles yarn is weaker than plied yarn, in general. It is always suitable for weft, but some singles yarn is too weak for warp. Pull on several strands of it together to see how easily it breaks if you are considering using a singles yarn for warp. The upholstery fabric we made was all of singles yarn, so you know from experience that it can work as warp.

If two or more singles yarns are then twisted together, the resulting yarn is called a **plied yarn.** Plied means twisted. A plied yarn is stronger than a singles, and usually has more abrasion resistance. That makes it especially easy to deal with as warp.

In addition to regular yarns, either single or plied, there is a great variety of novelty yarns. They are described by such fascinating names as loop, snarl, gimp, flake, and slub. Generally these are yarns with thicker and thinner areas. They will always work well as weft. But if you want to use a novelty yarn as warp you will need to test its strength by pulling to see how easily it breaks, and also by putting it through your reed or rigid heddle to see if the lumps pass without shredding.

Regular yarns are described by numbers. If you walk into a yarn store for your purchase, these numbers might not mean too much to you, as you can judge the size visually. But if you are ordering yarn by mail, you need some understanding of the numbers. The number looks like a fraction. The upper number is the count, and the lower number is the ply.

Count is a number indicating the thickness of the singles yarn. It varies from one fiber to another, but in general is calculated on weight as related to length, telling how much length of this yarn makes one pound of weight. So the bigger the count, the more length there is in a pound. That means the bigger the count, the thinner the yarn. A five-count yarn is quite a bit thicker than a 20-count yarn.

The lower number of this fraction-like size description is the ply. A 2 indicates that two strands of that size yarn are twisted together. So a 5/2's yarn is two strands of five-count yarn twisted together. That's a

Singles   *Two-ply*

much thicker yarn than a 20/3's, which is three strands of 20-count yarn.

You don't need to memorize just how big each count of yarn is, especially since it would be different with each fiber. But this general ideal of how the system works will be useful.

Sett

Your sett (how close you space the yarn) depends on the thickness of the yarn you plan to use, the weave structure you have chosen for the project, and the stiffness or pliability you want in the finished fabric. I'd call that a very practical consideration.

Different weave structures require different spacing. If the warp is widely spaced, the weft will pack down and cover the warp, so the finished fabric will show only the weft, making a weft-faced or weft-predominant fabric. On the other hand, if the warp is spaced very closely together, then the weft cannot pack down and you end up with a warp-faced or warp-predominant fabric.

Another aspect of the weave structure that will influence the sett is the length of weft skips in the weave. Plain weave has the weft going over one, under one. But in a twill where the weft goes over two warp ends then under two, the fabric will need a little closer spacing in order to end up as substantial cloth. A weave with weft skips of five threads will require even closer spacing.

The stiffness of the finished fabric depends largely on how tightly packed the threads are. Closer spacing will lead to firmer or stiffer fabric, while looser spacing leaves the fabric more pliable or more drapeable.

In deciding what sett is appropriate for a particular project, ask yourself these questions:

1. Do I want to end up with a weft-faced, balanced, or warp-faced weave?
2. If I wrap the warp yarn I intend to use around a ruler, and make the spaces between the wraps of yarn the appropriate size for the weave I will use, how many wraps are in 1″ of the ruler? This is the number of ends per inch to use as the warp sett. Pay close attention to how much space is between yarns:
   a) A space of three to six yarn widths will give a weft-faced weave if beaten hard, or a very loose balanced weave if beaten gently.
   b) A space of one yarn width is correct for balanced plain weave.
   c) A space of half a yarn width is correct for twill weave, basket weave, or any other weave where the weft skips two or more warps.
   d) Yarns touching each other with no space between are half the number of ends per inch to use for a warp-faced weave. Count them and then multiply by two.

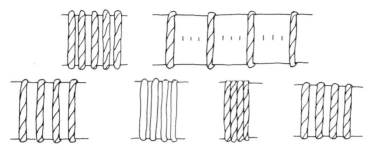

Wrap your warp yarn around a ruler, and visualize how the weft will pack in with different spacings. This can help determine an appropriate sett.

These are general rules of thumb and will get you very close to the correct sett. But they take into account only the size of the yarns and the weave structure. You will need to make slight adjustments for a tighter or a more pliable fabric. Weave a small sample first before you take on a large project, and wash the fabric before you judge it.

And, while the weave and the size of the warp yarn are of primary importance in determining sett, the nature of the warp yarn should be taken into consideration also. Do not use a sticky, fuzzy, or hairy yarn in a close sett because the yarns will stick to each other and make it hard to open the shed. These yarns make acceptable warp if they are sett far apart, however, so the fine hairs of adjacent ends don't tangle when they pass each other as the shed changes.

Pull-in

As you weave, you will find that the fabric will pull in, and not end up being as wide as you threaded it in the reed. This is normal—it's not something you did wrong! How much it pulls in depends on the weave structure and the stiffness of the weft yarn. Plain weave pulls in least, while weaves where the weft skips more than one warp end will pull in more. The longer the skips, the more the pull-in. Stiffer weft yarn will cause less pull-in than soft weft yarn. Linen, for example, causes little pull-in, while soft cotton causes a lot. Generally, you can guess at one to two inches total width loss due to pull-in.

But don't forget that shrinkage of the finished project when you wash it may also decrease your cloth. The only way I know to predict shrinkage precisely is to weave a sample and then measure it before and after you do whatever finishing processes you plan to use. Finishing should at least include washing.

A soft wool twill fabric is trimmed with hand-knitted bindings in this man's sweater vest by Lou Cabeen.

Take-up

Pull-in happens because the weft thread that you insert as a straight piece of yarn gets forced into a serpentine path as it passes over and under the warp ends in the cloth. The same is true of the warp ends—as soon as the cloth is off tension the warp ends are free to bend into a serpentine shape as they pass over and under weft threads. This is why when you unravel fabric, every thread is crimped. This crimping in the finished warp is called **take-up.** It takes up more length to crimp than to lie straight. (Remember ninth-grade plane geometry? The shortest distance between two points is a straight line.) Like pull-in, take-up depends on the weave structure and the stiffness of the warp, and shrinkage is another consideration beyond take-up. Allowing about ten percent extra warp length for take-up usually covers it.

Loom allowance

Your warp will also need extra length for **loom allowance.** You use up some length tying the warp ends onto the bar of the cloth beam and onto the bar of the warp beam. And on the floor or table loom, weaving has to stop when the bar of the warp beam is about 6″ behind the back harness, where it restricts the movement of the harnesses too much to continue weaving. On a rigid heddle loom, weaving has to stop when the back beam runs out of warp. From the knots at that point to the last pick of weaving is at least 12″ and probably more, depending on the particular loom you are using. You have to expect to throw away that much yarn. On a floor loom that's generally about ¾ of a yard of warp. When you figure out your needed warp length, you need to plan on throwing away this much. (These throw-away ends are called **thrums,** and some weavers go to great creative lengths to figure out uses for them.)

How much yarn do I need to buy?

How much will you need to buy? That depends on the sett, the width of the finished product, and the length of the warp. With these three pieces of information, you can figure out how much yarn to buy. Use this formula:

$$\times \frac{\text{number of ends per inch}}{\text{inches of width of the finished product plus } 1''\text{-}4'' \text{ for shrinkage and pull-in}}$$

= total number of warp ends needed

$$\begin{array}{r} + \\ + \end{array} \frac{\text{length desired for the finished product}}{\substack{27'' \text{ loom waste (or whatever your loom requires)} \\ \text{take-up and shrinkage}}}$$

= total warp length

$$\times \frac{\text{total number of ends needed}}{\text{total warp length}}$$

= total yards of warp yarn you need to buy

Weaving yarn is usually sold by the pound, not by the yard, but mail-order yarn suppliers and most good weaving shops will tell you how many yards per pound there are in each type of yarn, so you can convert this yards figure to a pounds figure.

That's how to figure out how much warp yarn to buy. You'll also need to buy yarn for the weft. In addition to knowing how many ends per inch you want in the warp, you will need to have an idea of how weft-predominant or warp-predominant the finished fabric should be.

You'll be amazed at the variety of different fabrics possible on even the simplest looms. This ribbed vest by Sharon Alderman is a fabric called "Bedford Cord". Search your library for more weaving books—the possibilities are endless!

How densely packed the weft is is expressed in terms of **picks per inch** or **p.p.i.** This is the number of crosswise threads in one inch of length of the woven cloth. To figure out how much weft yarn to buy, use this formula:

$\times$ width of the cloth (in inches)
$\times$ picks per inch
length of the finished project (in inches)
_____
= total inches of weft needed

Total inches of weft needed $\div$ 36 = total yards of weft needed

Use the yards per pound information for your particular yarn to figure how many pounds you will need to buy.

Choosing the Right Loom
For Your Needs

Though all looms work pretty much the same, there are still enough differences in them to make you want to consider carefully which kind of loom to buy before you rush out and spend your money. You not only want a good deal in quality per dollar, you also want the model that is most suited to your needs. You don't want to buy (and pay for) features that you won't use. So what are the features that you will use?

Perhaps after completing several projects, you have an idea of what kinds of projects you want to devote yourself to. For example, it took me only one handwoven rug to know that lighter-weight fabrics were what I wanted to make. So I didn't need the heaviest, sturdiest loom available. If you *do* like to weave rugs, you will need a loom that has heavy enough harnesses to make a good shed against heavy tension, and one that is sturdy and heavy enough to stand up to the very hard beating that weft-face rugs need. If a rug is not tightly beaten it will not last long, and it must be made of very sturdy materials.

Clothing fabrics, on the other hand, need a lighter beat in order to be flexible. Hard beating makes fabric stiff. The fibers themselves are less stiff and sturdy, too, so a lighter-weight loom will make quite satisfactory clothing.

If you don't know at this point what kind of objects you may want to limit yourself to, you will probably want to buy a fairly sturdy loom. But you might not want to spend the extra dollars to buy the very sturdiest, heaviest rug loom.

In addition to the weight of goods you will want to concentrate on with this loom, you also need to consider what width you will require. Most objects can be pieced from narrower strips. You usually don't really need as wide a loom as you first think. Factory looms commonly weave 45″ to 48″ wide, so we are used to thinking that we need that much width to make clothing. But we have made both a jacket from a commercial pattern and a top without a commercial pattern. So you know you can make clothing on a small loom. I've woven a lot of clothing on a 20″ loom. Now that I have a couple of bigger looms, I usually find that a width slightly wider than half my hip measurement works well. That allows me a front piece and a back piece, and it's ample width for one wide sleeve, too.

Pile rugs are easy to piece from narrower pieces, too, but flat-weave rugs are harder. Of course it can be done. The coverlets that our colonial ancestors wove were flat patterned cloth that always had a seam up the middle. Matching the complex pattern across this seam was difficult, so sometimes they didn't match too well. Somehow that seems perfectly acceptable in colonial coverlets, but you will have to decide how acceptable it is for your planned projects. But before you lay your dollars down for a wide loom, do a little creative thinking about how you could make do with a narrower loom. You may find you don't really need as much width as you thought.

Another pressing question when buying a loom is how many harnesses you want. If tapestries are what fascinate you, look carefully at a tapestry loom or a simple upright frame loom. Do you really prefer to concentrate on color and texture with a simple weave structure, or is complex weave structure a big love of yours? I know far more people who are content to weave on two or four harnesses all their lives than people who really use more. But I'm a complex structure nut, and I couldn't stand to have fewer. My first loom had eight harnesses (after I learned on rented four-harness looms), but since I got a 20-harness loom I've hardly once used fewer than 15! That's extreme behavior, but you do need to assess what fascinates you and what doesn't, and aim your loom purchase at your own idiosyncrasies.

Besides the type of finished product you will want to weave, the loom also needs to fit your body. When you buy a car, don't you sit in the driver's seat to see if the seat can be adjusted well for you? Well, a loom needs to consider that, too. If you are going to weave wide fabrics, sit at the loom and throw a shuttle the full width of the beater. You will have to reach at least 6″ to the right, throw the shuttle, and then reach 6″ to the left without changing your seating (just leaning side to side). Could you do that for an hour without hurting your neck and back? Unless you are a lot bigger and stronger than I am, a loom wider than 48″ may be a problem.

Consider a loom bench or stool when you consider the loom. Sitting on the bench, the front beam should just clear your bent, hanging elbow. If the beam is higher, you will find your elbows in the way all the time. If it is much lower, your neck and back will hurt from bending over too much. Of course you can adjust the bench or stool height to make this relationship right. Be sure you can reach the treadles comfortably when you have the stool-to-front-beam relationship right.

And when you buy a car, do you consider whether it will fit in your garage? If your house was built in 1917 like mine was, you'd certainly better consider this important question! Where will you use your loom? Will you be able to allow a foot of free space on each side and at the back of the loom? You will be reaching out with the shuttle in hand, and you don't want to scrape your knuckles. You will be walking to the back of the loom to fix broken warp ends, as well as to dress the loom. Will the size of loom you want fit into the space you have? I know several devoted weavers who have answered this by building onto their space to accommodate the loom, but you will want to at least weigh the alternatives first.

Many of my students have lived in small spaces and have needed a loom that folds when not in use and fits into a closet. There are several looms available to fill this need.

And now we get to the bottom line—can you afford the loom that suits all these needs? Don't forget you will need a few reeds, some shuttles, a warping frame or mill, and a few other things. Some of these can be improvised or added later, but do assess what you will need for your first few projects before you spend your last cent.

A Resource Guide

As you learn to weave, you'll find that your local weaving shop will be an invaluable source of information, advice, inspiration, equipment, and further lessons. Look in the Yellow Pages under "Crafts", "Weaving", or "Yarns". If there is no weaving shop in your area, there are a number of excellent mail-order companies dedicated to selling handweaving equipment, books and yarns, too. You can find current listings in these magazines:

Handwoven, 306 North Washington, Loveland, Colorado 80537. $18.00 for one year (5 issues). Lots of weaving projects with instructions, articles, book reviews, weaving news and events. Write and ask for a free sample copy, or use the card that you'll find in the back of this book.

Shuttle, Spindle & Dyepot, 65 LaSalle Road, West Hartford, Connecticut 06107. $18.00 for one year (4 issues). This is the membership publication of the Handweaver's Guild of America.

Weaver's Journal, P.O. Box 14238, St. Paul, Minnesota 55114. Articles of historical and technical interest, some projects as well.

Sources for yarns used in this book

If you can't find these yarns or a good substitute in your local yarn shop, write to the manufacturer for mail order information or the name of a dealer in your area.

Aurora Silks. Cheryl Kolander, 5806 N. Vancouver, Portland, OR 97217.
Borgs of Lund. Glimakra Looms 'n Yarns, 1304 Scott Street, Petaluma, CA 94952.
Crystal Palace Yarns. 3006 San Pablo Avenue, Berkeley, CA 94702.
Eaton Yarns. The Craftskellar, Marymount College, Tarrytown, NY 10591.
Gerald Whitaker. Box 172, Niagara Falls, NY 14305.
Harrisville Designs. Harrisville, NH 03450.
Henry's Attic. 5 Mercury Avenue, Monroe, NY 10950.
Lily Craft Products. B. Blumenthal, Box 798, Shawnee Mission, KS 66201.
Plymouth Yarns. 500 Lafayette Street, Bristol, PA 19007.
Schoolhouse Yarns. 25495 S.E. Hoffmeister Road, Boring, OR 97009.
School Products. 1201 Broadway, New York, NY 10001.
Wilde Yarns. 3737 Main Street, Philadelphia, PA 19127.

Some weaving equipment manufacturers

Write for their literature and the name of a nearby dealer where you can see their looms and other equipment.

AVL Looms. 601 Orange Street, Box H, Chico, CA 95926. Floor looms.

Beka, Inc. 542 Selby, Box H, St. Paul, MN 55102. Rigid heddle and floor looms.

Dorset Looms. Box 520-H, Stillwater, NY 12170. Free brochure. Floor looms.

Gilmore Looms. 1032 N. Broadway, Box H, Stockton, CA 95205. Free brochure. Floor looms.

Glimåkra Looms. 1338 Ross Street, Box H, Petaluma, CA 94954. Rigid heddle, tapestry, and floor looms.

Harrisville Designs. Box H, Harrisville, NH 03450. Catalog. Looms and loom kits.

J-Made. Box 452-H, Oregon City, OR 97045. Floor looms. Send $1.50 for catalog.

Kessenich Looms. 7463 Harwood Avenue, Wauwatosa, WI 53213.

LeClerc Corporation. Box 491-H, Plattsburgh, NY 12901. Rigid heddle, table and floor looms. Write for free catalog.

Loomcraft. Box 65-H, Littleton, CO 80160. Free brochure.

Louet. Box 70-H, Carleton Place, Ontario K7C 3P3. Free catalog. Table and floor looms.

Mountain Loom Co. Box 182-H, Curlew, WA 99118. Table looms.

Macomber Looms. Box 186-H, York, ME 03909. Write for catalog. Floor looms.

Norwood Looms. Box 167-H, Fremont, MI 49412. Send $1 for color catalog. Floor looms.

OR Rug Company. Lima, OH 45802. Send $.25 for brochure, Floor looms.

Schacht Spindle Company. P.O. Box 2157-H, Boulder, CO 80306. Send $2 for color catalog. Frame, rigid heddle, table and floor looms.

Sievers Looms. Indigo Road, Washington Island, WI 54246. Table and floor looms, plans, and kits. Send $2 for catalog.

Tools of the Trade. RFD HH, Fair Haven, VT 05743. Table and floor looms. Free brochure.

Some additional reading

Atwater, Mary Meigs. *The Shuttle-Craft Book of American Handweaving.* Coupeville, Washington: HTH Publishers, 1951.

Black, Mary E. *New Key to Weaving.* New York: The MacMillan Publishing Co., 1957.

Collingwood, Peter. *The Techniques of Rug Weaving.* New York: Watson-Guptill, 1968.

Garrett, Cay. *Warping All By Yourself.* Loveland, Colorado: The Handweaver Press, 1974. Interweave Press, distributor.

Kurtz, Carol S. *Design For Weaving, A Study Guide For Drafting, Designing and Color.* Loveland, Colorado: Interweave Press, 1985.

Redding, Debbie (Deborah Chandler). *Learning to Weave With Debbie Redding.* Loveland, Colorado: Interweave Press, 1984.